PORTS, POSTS
AND
PARKINSON'S

So you think you know me?

TONY FORD

authorHOUSE®

AuthorHouse™ UK
1663 Liberty Drive
Bloomington, IN 47403 USA
www.authorhouse.co.uk
Phone: UK TFN: 0800 0148641 (Toll Free inside the UK)
    UK Local: 02036 956322 (+44 20 3695 6322 from outside the UK)

Published by AuthorHouse 01/15/2021

ISBN: 978-1-6655-8345-9 (sc)
ISBN: 978-1-6655-8344-2 (e)

So you think you know me?

Dedicated to those I have loved, been loved by, and believed by, and none more so than my greatest supporter, my father, John. A bridge called love is often a rickety bridge but nonetheless still a bridge, so never stop crossing.

INTRODUCTION

They say there is a book in all of us, and that is probably true, but the critical issue is what to write about, and will anyone want to read it? Like many people, I have always thought about producing an international bestseller, but that means a dedicated period of scribbling down and fine-tuning a polished, finished book with little else to do, and for those who know me, that's simply not me. The two things which draw us to any book are ultimately the cover design and a catchy or clever title, and that's why this venture has taken eight years to bring to publication. Time is a great virtue, and although I'm in my late 50s, I still struggle to dedicate time to those who deserve more from me, but a life with set targets has never been the answer, and I suppose when it's ready, it's ready.

So what's this book about? I'm not sure at times, but maybe I am just afraid to admit that life is passing me by. I still have so much to do, but more importantly, I remember when life was simple, hard, but joyful.

I guess I have been lucky, blessed with an upbringing that was often out of the ordinary, but if I were to fall off my perch tomorrow, it could only be said, 'He did well.' I cannot confess to being a master with words or grammar, but the following is what it was, and what it is today, travelling from a sixties boyhood through family setbacks, a career in the Royal Navy, a diagnosis of Parkinson's disease (PD) at age 50, and the challenge of holding it all together now, in later life. I owe so much to so many, but any life is precious, and leaving a mark on others, albeit something small, is hopefully noteworthy. Welcome aboard the roller coaster.

They think it's all over.
—Kenneth Wolstenholme

30 July 1966 is a day that will live long in the memories of many people, albeit of a certain mature age. It was the day that England beat the mighty West Germans 4–2 to win the football World Cup at Wembley, thanks to a very popular Russian linesman. Hence, the immortal words of Kenneth Wolstenholme describing a triumph not seen since, but still to the annoyance of Scottish friends, and the first memories. Long before a life of ups and many downs for a boy with scabby knees in knee-length flannel shorts, wondering why everyone was seriously drunk.

I had not long celebrated my fifth birthday, and I can remember the sense of a huge event happening—even in my home in remote Stonehurst, Ardingly, West Sussex, in deepest southern England. I could sense from the battered black-and-white television set balanced on the sideboard that something monumental was happening just up the road in the capital. And looking back for both the country and myself, it was a day to remember.

I knew it was a Saturday, as the TV was on. It was only ever really on for sport on Saturdays. Any other day, we would have been outside enjoying a childhood that you would struggle to get nowadays. In our country location, we climbed trees, we jumped streams, and generally, the sun always shone. No mention of global warming; just a normal, warm, lazy summer.

My father, John, was not at home, which was no real surprise on a hot summer's day. He was, and still is, a grafter, then an estate worker, who would already be out when I got up in the early morning damp. And he would not return until it was too dark to work, with no harking on about working thirty-five hours a week. Besides, it was July, and it was hardly ever dark in the south of England at that time. There was an ethos of work until completion, with tiredness ignored. I now know that he was still looking to find his place in the world order after completing his required two years of national service in the army. But it was not work that caused him to be missing that afternoon; he had indulged in some escapism during a rare day off given by the estate.

It was a day off for a unique reason—home nation England was battling it out to be the best team in the world against a mighty West German team, packed with power and talent. Whilst he was usually on the fringes of some heavy drinking friends, that day, he had been drawn in by the occasion.

He made it home to the front door, which was good going, as Stonehurst was a remote location. I can still recall a socially confused mess of a man stumbling through the garden gate; the positive result had loosened any inhibitions. Whilst personally bemused, my mother, June, was waiting to give him a welcome which would put a distinct perspective on things. Times were fraught at home, and even with being so young, I sensed that not all was well with my parents. The 1960s may have been swinging for some, but for the majority, making ends meet was tough, and rewards were in short supply. It was a tempestuous welcome in a tempestuous relationship, and one ultimately deemed to failure.

My father is now approaching his middle 80s, but he's blessed with much more youthful looks. Although small in stature, he remains a giant in my eyes, and conversation about Stonehurst always brings a smile. He remains a big figure in my life, and any father who fought for custody of his children and won the day in the 1960s should be given the utmost respect. We have been close, and we have been very apart throughout the last fifty-odd years, but we are both better people when we are close, and I would never jeopardise that situation.

Whatever happened back in those early years, he was my dad, and whatever happens in the future, he will always be there, always my biggest supporter.

It is ironic how my life has panned out, paralleled with events from those heady days at Stonehurst with the same associated pain and pleasure, but more so painful today, battling personal illness and family break-ups. I still have the most vivid dreams from that era at Stonehurst. Waking up feeling like a small boy again, very much afraid of the dark. Anyone who tells you that they are not afraid of the dark is a liar. We all fear the unknown, and maybe now it is the plethora of drugs I take for my Parkinson's disease causing such a reaction, or I would rather believe I have a guiding angel on my shoulder reminding me to not forget the simple things which make you smile and remember.

SON OF AN ORCHID GROWER

I am not sure how many people in the United Kingdom are the children of orchid growers, but surely few and far between; however, that is what is on my birth certificate. Born on the anniversary of Bastille Day, 14 July 1961, the first born of John William Ford (occupation: orchid grower) and June Ford (housewife) at Cuckfield Hospital, West Sussex. And to this day, people always ask, 'Where the hell is Cuckfield?'

Growing orchids does sound grand, and he did indeed help to grow orchids, but his job on the estate was not always as elegant as that. The immediate area around Stonehurst boasted some impressive houses, including the imposing Wakehurst Place. However, we lived nearby in a modest cottage rented from the estate. I remember it was very basic with a kitchen, a living room, and one sizeable bedroom and box room. It took a long time to get another bedroom to call my own, but like most things in my life, it was not to last long once it arrived.

Apart from the grandness of Wakehurst Place and the sparseness of our own home, the other thing I remember about where I lived was the depth of gravel on the paths. You seemed to sink into it as a small child, and of course it was noisy, and the gravel was always pristine and weed-free. Even today, I have some pathological fear of walking on the stuff.

Whilst classed as an orchid grower, my father was no more than a general hand, working on various parts of the estate depending on the season, other estate tasks wide and varied, and when the weather was kind and even pleasurable. As well as general gardening and grounds maintenance, I remember him going out to collect sphagnum moss that was used in the production of orchids. Sphagnum moss is prevalent in Sussex woodlands, and even today, I recall its musty smell. The job was challenging, and working without gloves would leave young, soft hands scratched, cut, and sore. He also filled the substantial tanks of water under the glasshouses that fed the orchids with the required humidity for sustained growth, and like the sphagnum moss, the abiding memory is of the unique smell. In fact, my early childhood was full of organic pongs.

Living the country life might be a dream for many, but back in the late sixties, life was hard in the extreme. And if it snowed, we were snowed in for days with no fresh supplies, and you simply got on with it without fuss. Even during fine periods of weather, we lived off the land, with the likes of rabbit, pheasant, and pigeon on the menu, as well as the trout he helped breed within the estate's watercourses. We ate what was available, and it could have been trout for breakfast, dinner, and tea, and so much so I cannot now bring myself to even look a trout in the face perched on a plate, let alone take a knife and fork to it. It is the same with rabbit, or 'underground chicken' as we called it in the Royal Navy. When I was away on patrol in submarines, especially during the early 1980s, before the onset of myxomatosis, underground chicken would be on the menu probably once a week, being both cheap and something even a naval chef could cook without too much thought. Quite simply, at times, I would prefer to go hungry.

It was an uninspiring and lonely time in my life, and I cannot remember a lot of love being in the house; sadly, lacking in attention with my dad always working and my mother not liking the solitude. Even when my dad was in, it was a quiet house. My parents never really spoke, apart from the times they would spark each other into an argument. I was used to quiet, and I was effectively a loner in my own house. I would go out and play by myself, but there are only so many times you can climb the same trees. Even when my sister, Jeannette, was born, we did not do much as a family, as money was in shorter supply than trout. It was a pretty soulless existence, and I could not wait to go to school to meet others. I did not have any friends at Stonehurst; they simply did not exist.

My personal friendships became even more important as my family, for what it was, crumbled. I am not sure of the exact sequence of events, but much at the same time as I was starting school, my parents' marriage disintegrated. Looking back over fifty years, there could have been a bit of scandal attached to circumstances, but I do not remember sensing it then or getting a tough time about it at school.

All I remember, she was suddenly gone, just walking out with my sister. There was never any inkling of me going with her. And suddenly I felt abandoned, but I was too young to understand relationships (and some would argue that to this day, I still cannot).

I was sheltered from a lot of what was said and done by my paternal grandparents, as my father's world collapsed about him. The feeling of being totally isolated as a child is something that remains with me, knowing that maybe your birth mother didn't want you, but we never had a bad relationship that I can remember, but her taking my sister and leaving me behind hurt. Being so young but remembering so vividly this episode endorses the feeling of being unloved and unwanted, and yes, even today, with maturity and understanding, forgiveness will never really be there, although I understand the need to move on.

All these years later and with sensible weighing up of the odds, I can understand where the difficulties in my parents' marriage came from, like so many others struggling to get a foothold in the midsixties and a time of poor employment. My father would work all hours and hard manual jobs, and my mother would be left with a tired shell of a man when work was finally complete. My father's meagre salary simply could not match up to the level of expectation of the finer things in life my mother wanted, not just for herself but the whole family. It was simply economics over time for one another. I have no doubt that they loved each other, and my father tried, I remember, patching things up several times, but the writing was on the wall. My father to his credit will always say that my mother kept us clean and smart and always well looked after.

His work was a physically demanding job and largely in a male-dominated environment. When he got the chance, he would spend time relaxing with his small circle of friends and workmates; I remember that never going down very well with my mother, even though he was hardly a regular with his heavier-drinking colleagues.

It would be totally unfair to solely blame my mother for the pain in my life, as for one so young, I knew nothing about relationships, and as stated before, some would challenge me to say I know nothing today and am hard to live with. It must have been tough living in the countryside without friends and distractions, boring to the point where you would start to question your own sanity. After being separated and ultimately divorced, my father picked up the pieces, and I owe him everything; he went without luxuries personally and fought in the courts for custody of my sister Jeannette and myself. There would be times to come where I would question his thinking, but I can honestly say he has never got it wrong.

It must have caused a bit of gossip, but what's done is done. At the time, I knew something bad had happened between them, but I could not work it out, being of such tender years. Whilst I can understand that it was a difficult marriage for both, with finances and resources in short supply, it was a theme which was to mirror in my own life later on. In hindsight, the breakup of my parents' marriage was a key point in my early years and ultimately was a positive influence, but at the time, the sense of loneliness was immense (something I have hidden from everyone, until now).

We all ended up living not that far from each other. Sussex is not a big county, but I cannot ever remember bumping into Mum after the split. I can only imagine the pain my dad was enduring, but for a quiet man, he has the heart of a giant. He's still not afraid to face up to things, calm and to the point, a quality sadly I have to admit I have not inherited. During this unsettled period, I was at primary school at Ardingly and living with my grandparents at nearby Highbrook; this focussed my young mind on seeking the friendships I craved. Things were going to be alright, even a day off school to watch the moon landing in 1969.

One of the friendships I had formed ended with tragedy. Timothy Taylor was a class friend who was friendly and so easy to get on with; he simply disappeared one afternoon and was later found drowned in the local reservoir. His lifeless body was found in the reeds, and the episode compounds my fear of water to this day; a small part of me would suggest I later joined the Navy to get over that fear, but I remain paranoid when my own kids are anywhere near water.

I also remember Neil Durrant from those early days at school. He could still be in Ardingly, as could Lindsay Drew, who was a girl I sat beside in class. There were others from those early days; however, I cannot recall their names, but I remember becoming more and more involved with people, and my social skills flourished over a bottle of milk provided each day, either preheated, being left out in the summer sun, or frozen by harsh winters, but always opened at the foil top by a blue tit. I was probably one of a few who applauded an ambitious schools minister called Margaret Thatcher, who withdrew free school milk, and I often wonder whatever happened to her.

I remember vividly that first day at primary school back in August 1966; the sense of fear was overwhelming for a small boy in short trousers and doubly worrying being met at the gate by the headmaster, a tall, imposing, sinister-looking Mr Stanley Teasdale. Stan took great delight in running a tight ship of a school and was always immaculately turned out and dressed akin to the cartoon character Dick Dastardly, from the *Wacky Races* cartoon series, and was rarely seen without his trademark black gloves. For some strange reason, he decided to call me Charlie Ford for the duration of my early school years, and who was I to argue? The man fairly scared the skin off me. He was definitely old school but only caned me once for throwing a snowball one winter's day; it missed the intended target spectacularly and instead took out the school kitchen window, showering the staff therein with ice, glass, and the piece of coal I nicked from the school heating store to give the projectile some oomph.

I remember thinking it was worth the pain, as I did not want anything to be said at home, for fear of further confrontation and almost certain punishment. I was never caned again, and unbeknown to that small boy in the midsixties, my education and life was getting a good start; in hindsight, Mr Teasdale and his small staff of teachers were top class. Some years later, in the late 1970s, on leave as a young sailor, I was shopping in nearby Hayward's Heath with my grandfather, and we ran into an obviously seriously unwell Stan Teasdale; we had both obviously changed. Gone was the sharply dressed sinister man, replaced by a friendly old gentleman who not only remembered me from school but admitted to checking up on my career.

I still hold dear his words on parting: 'Work hard, and anything is possible, Anthony.'

I walked away, never to see him again; sadly, he died a

few weeks later of cancer, and as I got to the car, it dawned on me for the first time in over ten years, he had got my name right. They always say that schooldays are the best in your life, and certainly my life was shaped in those early, memorable, happy days at Ardingly Church of England Primary School, and it is only now on reflection that things might have been a whole lot different, but for Miss Cobb, Mrs Parsons, and the unforgettable Stan.

On the few occasions I have been back to Ardingly, I have given my early years haunts a wide sidestep, and as previously mentioned, my early friendships have long gone. I have moved on and in truth have no desire to really look over my shoulder for what was a pleasure and pain period in equal measure.

THE POCKET BATTLESHIP

They say the best thing about being a grandparent is you can look after your grandchildren, fill them with junk food and drink riddled with artificial colourings and additives, then send them home to their unsuspecting parents to suffer the consequences. That's the normal drill, but from the outset, I have to thank my late grandparents, Winifred and Joseph Ford, for stepping up to the mark for me and Jeannette, a task undertaken with no complaint, when in truth they should have been winding down from an already busy life together. They instilled values in me that remain to this day, lost on me then but now with both sadly gone and with children of my own; oh yes, they did a decent job.

Having been a loner at Stonehurst, things suddenly became much more intense, and I found myself encouraged to come out of my shell; the highlight of the week was going to the local Youth Club that was run by the sparky Vicar Guy Bowden, who eventually became a canon, no small achievement for a small village man of the cloth. He was immensely well respected, but I do remember one half-term holiday when he came to serious grief confronting my grandmother, taking her to task about not attending church, as he was looking to increase attendance figures. He made the mistake of comparing her and my hard-working grandfather to the Rothwells just next door, but a lifetime apart when it came to religion. They were neighbours and regular churchgoers, where Ruby was the lynchpin of the church, and husband Harry was the church groundsman and tended to the church clock, which had to be wound each day.

I remember well as my grandmother made the vicar tea, he slipped into the conversation, 'It would be nice to see you at church, Mrs Ford,' and he got the reply swiftly back that 'you don't have to go to church to be a good Christian, Vicar.' It was never brought up with her again, to my knowledge; subject closed, as was the cake tin. At the Monday night Youth Club, with around six kids and the chastised member of the clergy present, there would be all manner of odd indoor sports, with competition fierce, even for the likes of shove halfpenny with regular cheating rife, Vicar included. I suddenly realised that winning was everything, and being competitive was important, and as a result to this day, I remain a seriously bad loser. I can only blame that on my religious learnings at Highbrook.

My grandmother was an avid armchair fan of most sports and totally engrossed when major events were on. She took a fanatical interest in the new television boom when sports appeared in the 1970s. Tennis and snooker were her favourites, and as a proud Brit, Virginia Wade winning Wimbledon in 1977 was a red-letter day for her. It was a fantastic script made just for her, and it gave me much joy to see her so happy; she deserved it. In her early life, she had been in service at Windsor Castle and was a fierce defender of the Royal Family, and as it was the Queen's Jubilee year, Virginia Wade had won it for the Queen. Despite not often partaking, the port and lemonade were out that day in good measure. The other notable aspect of that memorable day was my uncle's description of Virginia Wade's very worthy opponent, Betty Stove, a description best left censored here; suffice to say, a great deal of bricks would be needed.

My grandmother loved to back the underdog, especially in tennis, and would frequently leap up out of her chair to cheer them on. She enjoyed Arthur Ashe winning in 1975, as he was a massive underdog and, of course, had overcame a lot of racism to do so, which I remember was rife during that decade and detested by her. She also enjoyed Stan Smith winning in 1972, as he was a gentleman who never used bad language. He also won it from an unseeded position: a gentleman and an underdog, nothing better for her. She would have loved Andy Murray winning; sorry, Andy, but a Brit first and foremost in her eyes.

The serious downside during Wimbledon fortnight was that she loved sport more than she loved cooking during these times, as she would sit glued to the television, and the men of the house, my grandfather, Uncle James, and myself, had to fend for ourselves. It was not easy, and I often found myself in the back of the car outside a local pub with a bottle of Coca-Cola and crisps, whilst the others old enough had lunch inside, as nothing was on offer at home, save a fifth set tie-break. It really was that bad; she just sat there and watched her beloved sport; fending for ourselves was disappointing, as she was a terrific cook, a proper cook, and she made us meals that could never be called pre-prepared.

She learnt how to cook at Windsor Castle, and we benefitted from that (well, we did when the tennis was not on).

As well as Virginia, Arthur, and Stan, her other tennis hero was Jimmy Connors. She liked him despite him having a bit of a nasty side to him and being an American; however, that liking of an anti-establishment hero did not stretch to wrestling. Saturday afternoons waiting for the football scores to come in was filled with the sound of Kent Wharton and wrestlers from across the country. She adored the Royal Brothers, and not because of their name but because they were good, clean-cut boys who obviously cared for their mum. Her liking for them was matched entirely by the dislike she had for Mick McManus, a horrible cheat and panto villain, of course.

She also got seriously into the snooker television boom, and after years of watching it on a black-and-white screen, I decided to treat her to a colour set, as I thought she would enjoy it more. I was working in the Royal Navy by this time and had a bit of cash, so I went to the local television dealership and bagged the latest and best colour set I could find. We got it duly installed and with Grandfather in tow took to a beer in the British Legion club some miles away in Danehill and left her watching snooker in glorious colour.

When we arrived back home, the snooker was back in black-and-white, as she did not like this innovation; she just wanted what she was used to and had turned the colour off. The following two weeks until pay day, I remember being totally skint, after paying for that television, and wishing I had asked the customer first what was needed. She did eventually accept the all-new John Logie Baird concept with colour, and the vigil for two weeks camped in the armchair continued.

Without doubt, my grandmother was the biggest positive in my life and the powerhouse of the family; everybody loved her. She was first up in the morning, and you didn't need an alarm clock, as you heard the Raeburn cooker being stoked up at 6 a.m.

Far from moaning about life, my grandmother embraced it and enjoyed being the homemaker, something my sister and myself really needed at the time. Her energy was limitless, and she did all this despite being born with only one lung and cutting its usefulness by smoking, which was still popular in the 1970s.

Whilst my grandmother was the engine room when I was growing up, my grandfather repaid her when she was dying. He was a forester at this time, and had worked with his hands all his life, but he tended to my gran in a totally caring and gentle way, belying his rustic appearance. He washed, dried, and styled her hair and bathed her with a soft touch, so as not to inflame the deep pain she was clearly in. He did everything he could for her. It was a solid marriage, a good marriage, and a real partnership in sickness and health. I was fortunate to see their later marriage close at hand, and my time at Highbrook with them is a memory which will never fade. Before the age of 11, I could stand up and do things other kids couldn't begin to comprehend; my grandfather believed that even an 11 year-old boy should pitch in and work.

As well as being in the Home Guard and farming during the war, my grandfather could have been classed as a jack of all trades, who would even turn his hand to milking cows on a casual basis when money was needed. His real love was the outdoors, and my memory will remain of a woodsman who worked long hours and always had a kind word and a smile for everyone.

Having been self-employed most of his life, my grandfather always had to deal with tax affairs, and that worried him. Every year, he would get a letter from the Inland Revenue, and it was a massive thing, as he thought he was going to get caught out for underestimating his income over the years. Cash was the order of the day in his business dealings, and he would settle up what he had to settle up, but his sense of underpaying the tax man troubled him so much that when he was about to retire, he wrote to the Inland Revenue, outlining his figures. He was well into his seventies by then but wanted affairs on an even keel; he also wanted to sleep without worry as he stopped working to concentrate on my ailing grandmother. I clearly remember the A4 envelope appearing with the chilling OHMS logo landing on the door mat and the pained look on his face. He needed not to have worried, as inside was a Guide to Retirement, a letter wishing him well, and a refund cheque for three hundred pounds, a princely sum at the time. Honesty and a great Christmas had come to the Ford household.

Whilst my grandfather had his own worries and cared for a failing wife, he made sure I was given responsibility from a tender age. I helped him during hay season by driving the tractor; I also used a chainsaw to fell trees and operated a bench saw, at times with a total disregard for health and safety criteria, but they were great times, and I grew up fast in a man's world.

During my stay at Highbrook, I failed my 11+ (or, rather, I never completed my 11+, as I fell asleep during the exam after playing football late the night before). Looking back, failing that exam did me a favour, as I ended up at a school that was not so strong on academics but outstanding for sporting opportunities. Little did I know that a minor setback would have such a massive boost later in my life.

Anyone visiting Highbrook would be taken aback by its charm, peace, and mixture of houses. In the mid-1970s, it had its share of interesting residents, and the endearing thing was that it didn't matter whether you were rich or poor; everyone knew everyone and helped each other.

The biggest celebrity resident, for the want of a better description, but also a likable, down-to-earth gentleman, was Reginald Leathes, a retired commandant of the Royal Marines. With an upright posture, pencil moustache, and military bearing, Reg was quite a man; he always had a story to tell about his exploits, and as my grandfather cut his expansive lawns, I would hear about his military exploits, and my inkling for a career at sea was being germinated. Some years later, I applied to join the Royal Navy and needed three character references. It was simple; I chose our milkman, David Allan; the father of a school friend, and of course Major General Reginald Carteret de Mussenden Leathes (Retired), Order of the British Empire, Royal Victorian Order, and Companion Order of the Bath. At my induction interview, I remember a very domineering officer asking if I was taking the piss, as you do not put the commandant of the Royal Marines alongside a milkman. It seemed sensible to me, as that was the diversity I grew up with (Dave would probably have a differing view, I am sure).

At just sixteen, I was accepted in the Royal Navy as a junior radio operator second class and delighted my grandparents, especially the pocket battleship, my grandmother, surprisingly, as she had lost all her brothers on active service in the space of a week or two during World War II. The Royal Navy as a career choice gave her pleasure, and I was truly proud to carry on the family tradition. The Submarine Service was drawing me in. I did worry about her fears for me, but she was a patriot, a Royalist, and hated anyone who was against that. She was a true-blue Conservative who thought Margaret Thatcher could put things right, and she hated the anti-establishment. She had little time for Trades Union people and disliked with a passion National Union of Mineworkers leader Arthur Scargill and the Post Office Union's Tom Jackson.

She was a huge figure in my life, a giant, and Highbrook Parish Church was packed at her funeral, the biggest attendance for many a year. Not only had she helped and loved me, but she had helped and loved a great deal of people during every part of her full and wonderful life, including people from the Royal household, High Court judges, and Members of Parliament; however, to me she was simply and importantly my nan.

That was only time I had seen my grandfather cry; he was lost and alone, and I remember seeing the pain in his eyes. Outside the church at Highbrook, he turned and just uttered, 'Sorry, boys; I let you down.' Nothing was ever as far from the truth, as he gave everything to everyone without fuss and always with love.

During my early life, my grandparents were my parents, and my father knew that. There is no shame, and I owe everything to the three of them in equal measure; maybe that's a lesson for all of us in the way modern life often pans out. Even today, it's so normal for grandparents to bear the brunt of childcare, and yes, my dad at eighty still enjoys the 'daddy day care' tag but no doubt is inwardly delighted to see his charges returned. This chapter in my life has taken the longest to put to print, and I must admit it has brought tears to my eyes; even now, the memories of fun-filled summers remain as beacons which will never be extinguished until I return to Highbrook after my life is run.

MOVING ON

The third main period of my life again brought change, another challenge to a young mind, but it also drew me closer to my father, brought shared happiness through normal family life, but ultimately was to end in tragedy.

This period of my life is split down the middle of business and family. The business side of things centres squarely on Spalding Horticultural Company Ltd, now long gone of Swan Street, Spalding, the capital of the Lincolnshire fens. The family aspect revolved around a person I loved dearly, simply for her kindness and the love she expressed for everyone and especially for my father, who was happy again; the effect was there for all to see. That person was Lynda Beryl Gladman, who was to become my dad's second wife, a stepmother to my sister Jeannette, and an understanding ear to a shy and retiring boy. Lynn was simply perfect for my dad, understanding fully the needs of two young people, smart, and, yes, pretty, and once again proved that the male of the Ford dynasty could pick a looker and punch above their weight.

It was purely business that saw the family uprooted from the love and fun at Highbrook; we moved to Lincolnshire, a bungalow and flower nursery at Surfleet, a small village close to Spalding. Our stay at Highbrook had lasted just over five years, a time that shaped our lives and continues to do so even today. At about this time, my father fell in with Lionel Leonard. I'm not entirely sure how they met, but that is immaterial, as Lionel, to put it nicely, was a hard-nosed businessman, driven, and tolerated few, but he gave my dad the opportunity in life he sorely needed.

Lionel was very friendly with the legendary racing driver Stirling Moss, and in fact, Stirling had been his best man when Lionel married Jean, his lovely and caring wife, who sadly died in 2013 after surviving Lionel.

He was an ideas man and a hard-nosed one, at that. He knew what he wanted done, he was happy to impose on people, and he surrounded himself with doers. He was a thinker and wanted to be known as a thinker, whilst others got on with things. My dad was in his sights.

My father was a grafter, and Lionel used him as the lynchpin, as he would get things done without fuss. That can-do quality came from my grandfather, and I'd like to think it was instilled in myself during my time in the Royal Navy and now in the present. It is an old saying but relevant: 'If a job's worth doing, probably best done yourself.'

Lionel hailed from Scaynes Hill, also in leafy Sussex, and he noticed what people were spending their money on, especially when times were tough financially. Sussex remains an unbelievably beautiful county and is dominated by houses with extensive gardens; personal wealth is openly exhibited (at times, obscenely). Highbrook had been a classic case of the mixture of working class and retirees like Reg, my erstwhile commandant of the Royal Marines at the other end of the scale, typical and commonplace. You saw grounds where it looked like ten gardeners were needed. Even in a recession, people buy chocolate, as it is a comfort thing, and they also spend money on their garden, a fact not lost on Lionel.

Lionel picked up on this and then realised the buying public had few choices for spending money on their gardens. There were some garden centres around, but not many, unlike today; in the 1970s, supermarkets were still pretty basic, sticking to their usual offering of fresh food and cans of beans. The leisure market was not there in supermarkets, and whilst some might have sold a small trowel, that was about it.

Lionel realised that people planted a lot of flower bulbs in their gardens, and they paid a fortune for them at garden centres. He did his homework and even went off to where the bulbs were grown in Holland. He came up with the idea of putting ten bulbs in a pack, put a nice picture on the front, staple the whole thing together, and offer it for sale at a supermarket. He wanted to get the masses to buy them. It's taken for granted now, but no one had thought of it back then. Credit where due, he had the vision, and if you go to a supermarket today, there are thousands of garden products.

Lionel did not stick to the one idea, either; he brought gardening to everyone. He devised glasses and holders for hyacinth bulbs to be grown, for the little old lady living on her own in a small flat with a window box. He had many ideas, and businesses like the imported Dutch bulbs began to grow. The concept was simple but demanding work in those early days, as he had to travel to Lisse for the bulb auction to get the biggest profit margin; it made for a long, exhausting week. He was the ideas man, and of course he roped both families into doing the work; on the weekends when my dad would come home to Highbrook, we would all be involved in putting hyacinth bulbs in plastic holders and boxes. Whilst most people were out doing normal things on a weekend, we were subjected to the latest idea.

I think it fair to say that my dad just wanted to keep the wolf from the door and rebuild the shattered family, but Lionel had bigger plans; he had enormous plans, and to be fair to him, he saw them through. He established a base in two warehouses in Swan Street, Spalding, Lincolnshire, the capital of the Lincolnshire fens. One property had belonged to Bryant and May, the matchmakers, and this listed building became the home of Spalding Horticultural Limited Company Ltd. It was a good spot and had the attraction of a nearby public house, the Pied Calf, which conveniently opened early on an auction day.

They both worked long hours, but they started making friends and built a life. My dad was getting his hands dirty, something he still does today without drama, and Lionel worked hard at establishing contacts. The double act worked well, and a smile was there again as reward grew.

It was a hard life; they commuted from the south to Lincolnshire before moving there, and they would leave around four on Monday mornings so they could start trading at eight and buy and sell at the nearby flower auction. They would be buying and selling for a few extra pence, and the first aim was to get enough money to get home again on the Friday. It was close call a few times, but they always seemed to pull it off.

If they were short, work just continued, and they would

come home on a Friday night, shattered. Dad would flop on the bed for a couple of hours and then go out to the pub to catch up with news and come home and flop on the bed again. Meanwhile, we would still be hard at work downstairs with more bulbs in more pots.

If I were on holiday, I would travel up and stay with them; slowly but surely, they got things together and realised that their future lay in Spalding.

Before moving up, my dad stayed during the week in digs just outside Spalding in Pinchbeck, a nondescript village. He stayed in a welcoming public house, the Bull, which still stands. The landlord soon became 'Uncle Jack' and great company, and he looked after us all when we stayed. The temptation was obviously there at the end of the day for a pint, but rarely would it go beyond, as this was Lincolnshire, and people were up well before the rooster. Staying there did have a benefit, as pubs still closed in the afternoon, and occasionally the opportunity was there for a round of golf. To this day, I am still underwhelmed by the game, but being a caddy had its perks, with a mouth full of chocolate and a cold one from the bar stashed in the bag for the back nine. Jack was a skilful player, and because they were playing often, my dad could knock the ball around the very flat fenland course. Business took off and killed any aspirations of a career in golf, but another example of the love of sport in my family; strangely, in his retirement, my dad has never felt the urge to put club to ball, but even approaching eighty-three, I would not put it past him to dust off his bag if challenged, such is his competitiveness.

Spalding Horticulture's initial customers were largely market traders who would come in with a pile of cash and not worry too much about VAT and taxes; they had to be handled in a delicate manner, but Lionel could be a hard-nosed bastard in business with the best of them.

If he did not like someone, he would say, 'I don't like him, and after you take his cash, show him the door.'

One instance I vividly recall. One day, while I was at the warehouse, a dishevelled figure walked in; it was raining hard, as only it can in Lincolnshire. Flower bulbs have an earthy scent, and a warehouse full of them can smell really oppressive. This gentleman walked in, and his odour was stronger than any of the flower bulbs. He had not seen a bath in a few days, that was for sure; Lionel assumed he was a tramp and gave instructions to see him off the sales floor, akin to 'John, get that smelly sod out of here.'

That was not the Ford way; we'll talk to anyone who has the stupidity to stop and listen, so the sales charm kicked in with 'Yes, sir; what can I do for you?' The well-rehearsed presentation tumbled from my lips: 'This is what we do with bulbs from Holland: put ten in a pack etc.'

The now rapidly drying out gentleman duly responded, 'I'm extremely interested in that. I represent a new group of small supermarkets that is going to be based in Lincolnshire, Yorkshire, and the east coast of England; any chance we can buy a few cases to see how it goes?'

That fledgling supermarket was called Morrison's, and this gentleman was their main buyer, having been on the road for over a week. I'm unsure just how much money crossed the till over the following years, but suffice to say that well-known phrase of judging books and covers springs to mind; even offering a cup of tea in a chipped mug can often sway favour.

Lionel's style did have benefits, and his ideas and concepts led to several patents. He was fiercely protective. People would try and pinch an idea, but he would fight them. He would enjoy that as well. If he lost a few pounds, he didn't mind, as long as he got his point across.

He was determined and often hard-driven, and I'm not sure his confrontational approach was always good, but my dad rarely if ever said a word against him. They were the perfect team for each other: good cop, bad cop. Although my dad rounded off the corners, Lionel in short invented the wheel. Sadly, he died not long after making Spalding Horticultural Company Ltd a major success, and I can still see his smiling face and hear his bellowing laugh.

During this period, my father would spend the weekends with us at Highbrook, and that brought concerns to my dear old grey-haired nan. She was a naturally nervous person, and Dad's driving up and down the country each week worried her sick, as she saw the exhaustion in his face. During the late 1970s, when I was serving in the Royal Navy, there was a major train crash in Bangladesh, killing about a hundred passengers, on the same day I was returning from leave, taking the train to Petersfield in Hampshire. She called frantically to make sure I was okay and not involved in that incident. I don't know how many stops the train would have to make to reach the likes of Bangladesh, but it was nice to be looked out for. 'Oh, thank God you've called me back,' she said, and my grandfather just shook his head. No matter what he tried, he could not put her mind at rest. She could worry for everyone.

Not only travelling worried her; so did night banking of daily cash takings. The business in Spalding was cash-driven in those early days, and one Friday, after missing the bank closing, my weary father duly returned to Highbrook with pockets stuffed with a busy day's takings. It was a sizable amount of money, and he simply threw the cash on the bed and went to the pub. It was only a matter of time before grandmother gathered his clothes to wash and saw the stash of cash. She just about died on the spot and maintained a bedside vigil until my dad returned. He fell through the door and promised through a drunken haze never to do it again; to my knowledge, he never did.

The business took off with the boom in easy access gardening, with supermarkets and garden centres clamouring for market share, but it was never a get-rich-quick business. It was hard graft, and earnings were invested back into the business. Lionel moved to a house locally to Spalding, and my dad ended up at the Nursery in sleepy Surfleet village, six miles out from Spalding, which is home still to this day; they began growing their own flower bulbs and plants as a side line, with the glasshouses on-site. My dad loved it, as he had greenhouses full of plants and a team of ladies potting them for growing on within the glasshouses, and all became great friends to this day forty-plus years later.

It started off as a seat-of-their-pants business, but as it grew, they could not keep commuting, and Spalding was to become our new home.

I sampled travelling back and forwards to Sussex a few times. At that time, you could drive through the middle of London at four o'clock in the morning and have a pit stop in Golders Green, where we would stop at Grodzinski's, a Jewish bakery which was open all night.

You would get a great coffee, a real cup of coffee and a

freshly baked fantastic pastry and take a box away with you. The Jewish bakers were good people with friendly natures, and you would get shouts of, 'Morning, Tony; morning, John'; it was good to be accepted. My love of a good pastry continues today, but they were by far the best, and I would sneak one from the box in the back of the car whilst driving up the A1 road to Spalding and the start of a week's work.

Spalding was the horticultural capital of Britain; it still is, although less busy today. It was a small industry with cut flowers and spring bulbs, but it has grown, excuse the pun, to become a huge international trading industry, mainly with the Dutch connection. It supported the annual Spalding Flower Parade, when decorated floats adorned with tulip heads paraded around the town to massive crowds, and was also vastly important to other local businesses, but today, sadly, no more due to the decline in the industry. Spalding and its friendly exterior provided a base for family life, and I joined my dad and Jeannette there in 1974; my baby sis had come back a year after my mum left, so she had grown up through this period as well. My dad had fought and won custody of her, and even today, it's difficult for a father to gain custody, even in extreme circumstances, so to do it twice was quite remarkable and again speaks strongly for my father's inner strength not to accept the inevitable.

Moving to Spalding had to happen for the sanity of my dad, but it was with a heavy heart, as once again, I had just settled at a good school.

I had largely enjoyed my time at Ardingly Primary, but Oakhall School in Haywards Heath was a new school, with a real leaning towards sport; for the first time, I had the opportunity to be coached and play on a team. It was fantastic, and my continuing taste for competition was born. The one term at Oakhall School also sparked an interest, unwittingly, in cycling, as the school bus only ventured to Lyewood Common, some three miles up and downhill from Highbrook and home; thankfully, I never experienced Sussex's extreme winter weather on two wheels. There were a couple of tumbles. I remember heading to the bus on a bike with plenty of miles on the clock; one fall resulted in a trip to the dentist and a letter to my grandparents, asking why I attended school covered in blood (I had wiped a mixture of the red stuff and gear oil all over the glass entrance doors.

I rode back and forth to the school bus with Paul and David Bryant, identical twins, who were amongst the six local kids who went from our village to Oakhall. There was a sense of community then; we would pop off our bikes to visit Mrs Chatfield, who lived halfway between our start and end, and was well into her eighties. She lived by herself, enjoyed a quiet life, and was glad of the company, even if it was three rebellious kids. The twins and I would pop in and get a cup of tea; they would also smoke a Players Number 6, but I resisted the temptation to have a crafty fag. The thought of my grandparents discovering my misdemeanour and then belting me acted as a good deterrent.

Ma Chatfield would tell us stories of her family and growing up in poverty; she had a life of very few frills, but she was ultimately happy. She had tales of brothers in the Navy, and when she died, it was the end of an era, as she was the last of her family's line. She had a great outlook on life and was a bit of a social worker; she always said, 'What will be, will be. Live every day as if it were to be your last,' she would say, and 'Do at least one good thing for someone else and you will not go far wrong.' It was good advice, as there were highs and lows to contend with on the immediate horizon.

Before I started at Oakhall School, I was given a list of things to bring, including an apron for metalwork class, a subject I fancied a tilt at; to this day, I still enjoy the art of forge work, but that began with another classic from my grandmother. Whilst everyone went out and bought an apron, she of course made one, and it was a dog's bollocks of aprons. People would ask where it came from, and Nan became famous overnight, it seemed; she even took in a couple of orders, but on the downside, the school list also stated short trousers were optional for uniforms, and my grandmother decided that since my grandfather and father had gone to school in their shorts, I was to go as well. I attended school with about two hundred other boys, and I was the only one there in shorts. I went home after that first day, and it's the only time I can remember being angry with my gran. I told her in a distressed way, 'No more shorts.'

She must have known how seriously angry I was, as she agreed instantly and got me long trousers.

When we moved to Spalding, there was a new woman in Dad's life: his second wife, Lynda, or Lyn, as I knew her. Like his first marriage, this was brief, from 1972 to July 1976; however, that is where the similarities end, as it was a strong marriage until, sadly, Lyn died from Hodgkinson's lymphoma. She was a lovely person, dedicated to my dad, and taken from us all far too early.

Lyn had a fantastic nature, perfect for my dad, and was everything to him. She was caring, did the simple things like making sure everyone was looked after, and had a kind word when things needed sorting. Everyone who met her was instantly taken in with her warm and friendly nature. There was not a bad bone in her body, and she accepted me and my sister fully, and not just her but her mother Joyce and brother Chris. We were all accepted and loved, and it felt good before the loss.

So the mid-1970s saw my attendance at the Sir John Gleed Boys' School in Spalding, a big step up in my sporting life. It was a damned good school that was big on sports. It softened the blow of moving and losing friends, but I quickly made some new ones, including Dennis Smith, our neighbour across the road, who remains a good pal; we rarely meet up today, which is sad, as we were in lots of scrapes together as youngsters (and some best not mentioned in print, as the cases are probably still open). It was a time to flourish as a teenager and to catch up to modern ways after the dutiful time living with grandparents. I was growing up fast.

It is without question a big wrench for a young person to move schools and change homes; however, people from a military background kind of get used to it, but you still worry about being accepted, especially moving to a totally new area. North of London was a totally alien concept. Even today, I still feel connected to the south coast, and although I worked and lived in Scotland these past thirty years, I wish to return when my sun sets. But as of then, and for most of my immediate family now, the fens of Lincolnshire were home. It is a massive farming area due to the reclaimed nature of the land, with water levels controlled by drainage dykes, and pumps are a constant reminder that the whole area is thirteen feet below sea level. The people of Lincolnshire and the farming community are extremely down-to-earth and friendly. That said, they will tell you if they don't like you, and I had a bit of that when I first arrived at the Gleed Boys' School, but I was finally accepted.

Lincolnshire was a second chance for my dad. The business was still time-consuming, but family life became ordered and calm without commuting from the south; he was getting a bit of time to himself, and he deserved it. Things had taken off for Dad but then came to a shuddering halt with the news of Lyn's diagnosis. It was shattering news; hard to believe someone with such energy could be so seriously ill. She died in July 1976 at just twenty-six.

Lyn and my dad had just three and a half years together, but they were immensely happy years as a real family. They had married just before moving up from the south in 1972. The wedding took place on the Sussex/Surrey border, with the reception at a hotel; it was a bit strange to go to your dad's wedding, and my abiding memory is of sitting in the beer garden, polishing off several bottles of sparkling rose wine. For someone aged just twelve, my tolerance to alcohol was outstanding, compared anyway to a number of my immediate family, later comatose on the garden benches, and that skill set would stand me in good stead in the following teenage years of excess and the small matter of thirty-four years serving in the Royal Navy.

Children never happened for them, which was a shame now looking back, as Lyn would have been a loving mother, and despite my dad being a little bit more senior in years than her, they were perfect for each other. There is no way of saying it any differently: Lyn was everything my dad needed at that time in his life. She was a steadying influence and simply someone to come home to and love, better than returning to a room above the pub lounge and sitting there with a bit of paper, planning the next day.

Lyn died in 1976, just under a year before I joined the Navy. I wanted to see it through for her and be accepted into the service, as she had always encouraged me, like my grandparents before. At the time of her death, I remember I was in the middle of exams and distracted from her plight and my dad's constant visits to the hospital.

Of course, I knew she was ill, and I remember my dad coming into my bedroom early that fateful morning and simply saying, 'Your mum has died overnight, son; she's not in any pain anymore. Get yourself up and ready for school. Make sure you have something for breakfast.'

He made a few phone calls and trundled off to work. That was and is my dad, no sodding emotion, dutiful, no drama, but he was hurting inside. I wear my heart on my sleeve and am an emotional person, but my dad never shows his feelings, and respect is due.

There was a service for her at a crematorium near Gatwick and her family home, and my dad still visits there on a regular basis to lay flowers on a small plot, as he does similarly at the Highbrook graves of my grandparents. It has become a ritual for him. It is nearly forty years, but he has never wavered from doing it, such is his loyalty.

After the shock of Lyn's death, our fantastic circle of friends in Lincolnshire closed ranks around us as well as family and friends from down south. One of those kind people was a previous girlfriend, Maureen Penfold, who took up the reins and helped run the family home and look after us. Maureen, along with a lot of people, helped to put the family unit back on a level footing. My dad just did what he did best and got on with working all the hours available.

Lyn was the third maternal figure in my life. It was a new beginning for my dad, my sister, and I, and although she was only with us for a brief period, much of what I have become is down to Lyn and her outlook on life. If she were alive now, she would be a Facebook or Twitter-type person, telling the world what was going on. Maureen would eventually bring renewed contentment to my dad, a happy conclusion after years of setbacks and an enduring love for each other; they married and she became a second stepmother, a different relationship for myself but equally important with the bonus of two younger brothers, Ben and Daniel, now both married with their own young families.

During this latest disaster to strike, it was strange not seeing my grandparents as much, and although my life was now away from them, I was to remain closer to them, as Junior Radio Operator Submarines A J Ford, D167542S, was about to defend the British Empire.

IN THE NAVY

When I joined the Royal Navy in 1977, I was based in Petersfield, just outside Portsmouth, and when I got weekends off or had leave, I would go back to Highbrook and stay with my grandparents. It was like being back home, and that included my laundry; even my socks were ironed by my diligent nan. I cherished those weekends, as the training was hard, stressful, and intense. I was suddenly making up for lost time and growing up fast, discovering the things Portsmouth had to offer after dark and the appeal of a regular wage and a uniform. Joining the Navy helped me become my own person; Lyn had encouraged me, as she knew it was something I really wanted to do. It was a seed that had been germinated by a grandmother and old Ma Chatfield's tales.

It was easier for me to think about joining the Navy, seeing my dad settled once again. I would not have thought about leaving if it had not been the case, but his home life was good again. The Navy reignited my competitiveness, and suddenly, winning was everything, as divisional pride was at stake and, moreover, bragging rights in the Navy, Army, Air Force Institutes (NAAFI). To this day, I hate losing at anything I play or do. You can lose with dignity, but I bloody hate shaking hands after a loss; it's not something I'm particularly proud of, but competing and winning is everything.

Things at home in far-off Surfleet during the early 1980s were largely unseen, as my career in the Royal Navy and the submarine service became all consuming. It was a busy period; during brief periods of leave, after being at sea for several weeks, I would head home to Surfleet with a full wallet. This was an advantage over a poorly paid land worker, and certainly cash in hand was a real bonus on a Saturday night on the town with the girls dancing around their handbags.

One of the first girls I fell in with was Carol Posey; I have no idea where she is now, but at seventeen, she was tall, very, very tall, and I was short in comparison. The local social event was the Friday night disco in a local village hall; the usual fare was a bottle of cider getting passed around and then a snog whilst waiting for a lift home. I had to stand on the railings to get a kiss due to the height difference. Carol was a stunner, great legs, and I think the main attraction was my southern accent; it was a bit different from the rest of the local boys.

I was once asked if I was from America with the accent, and even after living around the UK, it has not deserted me. Looking back, some of the land workers had never left Lincolnshire, and they had the mentality of farming, farming, and fuck all else. My friend Julian Snaith's dad always said that these people would die with millions in the bank rather than spend it. I remember getting some stick from my sister about Carol's height when quizzed by an inquisitive grandmother.

My sister took great delight in explaining the need for railings, to which my good Christian grandmother replied, 'Don't worry, son; they are all the same size when lying down.'

My grandfather was left choking on his tea at the response, and the subject of girlfriends was never raised again at Highbrook. Carol lived near my best friend from school, with a easy name to recall. Patrick Gotobed was the unfortunate person to have me as a best pal and a surname that always brought a snigger in class. He had his name legally changed to Lewis. Pat was a Wolverhampton Wanderers FC fan, and I don't know where the hell that came from, as they were not a popular choice back then, and as a farmer's son, Pat certainly had not been anywhere near bloody Wolverhampton.

It was a good time to join the Royal Navy; I had gone for a haircut the day before travelling to Torpoint for basic training, as my hair style followed the lead singer of the pop band the Sweet. My old man, with two years of national service, told me that it was still not short enough, and as ever, he was right.

When you enter the main gate of HMS Raleigh, a sprawling estate of buildings in Torpoint, Cornwall, where new-entry training is conducted, the routine is probably just the same today as it was on that sunny day in August 1977: You line up with your bags along with the other extremely nervous new recruits, and out trots a scary older uniformed figure with cigarette ash adorning his ruffled jacket. He barks in short order, 'Am I hurting you by standing on your hair, son?' and my immediate thought was the total waste of money spent only yesterday as another two pounds was about to leave my pocket with a trip to the base barber, who must have been in partnership with that old chief petty officer and his chain smoking habit.

That was just the start, and the realisation that this was bloody real suddenly hit me, and even the reassurance that six weeks sees you through the first part of training still left an empty feeling in the stomach; suddenly, Highbrook and Surfleet were a long way away.

Your accommodation had to be spotless, but thankfully, my grandparents' domestic training helped me do that with consummate ease. I was domesticated, and that helped with duties such as ironing, sewing on buttons, and endless hours bulling boots, a sadistic way of adding layers of polish to footwear and an art which I also soon mastered.

Of course, you had to do these things quietly, as if you were caught making a noise, you were out in the parade ground at 2 a.m. doing drills. It was cold, numbingly cold in the middle of winter, and the duty instructors demanded absolute respect. The Armed Forces today has changed greatly but, in many areas, not for the better. It is not the same now as it was then. It was a little brutal and designed to try and break you. It was six weeks of confinement, where you did not get any outside communication. There was no internet, no mobiles, and around three hundred souls for the one phone box. You live in the NAAFI club, and that was where the strangest things happened; even at that early stage, friendships are honed and made for life, even now, nearly forty years later.

You must go to church on Sunday, and there is no such

thing as being atheist, a nonbeliever, or a worshipper of the moon. In the Armed Forces, you must be something; you cannot be a nothing. I was sitting there, and Chief Petty Officer Simon Jeffrey asked me if I was Church of England.

I said innocently, 'Yes, what else is there?'

'Bit of advice, son; say that you are not that strong a believer. They will put you down as Church of Scotland; you get great tea and cakes there from the Jock Bishop, much better than the English crowd.'

I did as I was told; they asked, 'So you were raised near Brighton and you are Church of Scotland?' I just said I had a Scottish grandmother, so I found myself at the Church of Scotland on a Sunday, with a whole load of boys from London, who would have struggled to show you Glasgow on the map. The Church of Scotland chaplain loved the attendance, as everybody was encouraged to put their money on the collection plate for the church steeple fund, of which there was no sign, to this day. Even so, the cakes were bloody marvellous, and it was a small light relief on a Sunday after a tiring and painfully hard week.

When you start in the forces, you simply do not have a clue. You would walk around the base (well, actually run around it), saluting everyone. I saluted the chief one night and heard him say in a loud voice, 'I am in charge, and I know what I am doing; I'm not an officer.'

On day 1, you must declare if you use tobacco products or not; you got duty-free cigarettes at that time in exchange for special issued stamps that you were given every month. Those stamps got you eight hundred cigarettes on your paybook or the same value in 'tickler', the naval slang for smoking tobacco.

As I filled in the form, someone senior was on my shoulder, saying, 'You are a smoker, son,' and I replied, 'I'm not, actually,' to which the reply was, 'You are a fucking smoker, son, as of today.'

Everybody joining the Navy in 1977, it seemed, was a smoker or stamp trader. The cigarettes ended up getting sold somewhere, but I never asked.

I look back now and laugh; however, at the time, it was a frightening experience. I was sixteen, and it was a whole new world, one fixed telephone and three hundred people: no mobile phones, no internet, and no contact with anyone.

You are on your own bulling shoes, boots, doing anything blindly without question you were told to and getting involved in things set to push and push you even to a point you begin to self-doubt. Many fell by the wayside each day; the only consolation was the queue for dinner each evening got shorter.

Boxing is a sport I enjoy to this day, but in August 1977, it also formed some major concerns during those tender first six weeks. It was a specialised sport, and I thought I would do okay; Wayne Green was my nemesis, a likeable south London black boy, the same height (five feet, six inches) as me, but with an advantage: He knew how to box; he was outstanding and much better than me. You basically lined up smallest on the left, tallest on the right, and paired off. Wayne was never going to not stand next to me; he hit me twice, and that was enough. I later learnt he had become an ABA champion, somewhat restoring my self-pride.

There were quite a few black kids joining up in the 1970s, and one of them, John Kenwood, turned out to be a great pal; there were never any racial issues onboard ship, something I deplore to this day and have tirelessly campaigned against. He was known simply as 'Chalky' in those Jim Davidson days, and like others, we served with great affection. He was from Liverpool, as was his wife, and when she first came down to meet the boys in Plymouth, she got the shock of her life.

One of the lads, Tom Inglis, was from Southampton, and he walked into the bar very drunk and said, 'Alright Chalky, you black bastard.'

That, to Tom, was a friendly greeting, which was just as graphic to anyone black or white, but John's wife sank into her seat and asked who this was. Tom and Chalky were simply friends, and that was the humour of the day; it was not viewed as racist then. Chalky would dish it out as well, and everyone laughed and looked after one another, whatever colour your skin was or if you worshipped another planet or god, it mattered not a jot. There was no racism in the group, no bullying, just a group of guys trying to get through training, but that feeling was to last a lifetime, even today. A lot of stuff that has gone on since, in terms of people wanting compensation for racism in the forces, is totally without credence, as far as I am concerned. I never saw or heard anything at the time; we were all in the same boat, literally.

After a few days, we were a team; it was a bit like *An Officer and a Gentleman*; one guy who excelled at cleaning the shoes did that for the group, I was good at ironing, so I did that, but it was a hard regime. Even the way you talk changed; the Navy has its own language (or slanguage), and you are encouraged to learn it and think like a sailor.

You would have all your kit laid out, and if one member

of the class were not up to scratch, all the kit was trashed. It was the old polish-the-floor-with-a-toothbrush punishment, but you sucked your teeth and got on with it. That sense of equality and team thinking remains now as was embedded in me then. You learn tolerance, as some of the boys came from differing academic backgrounds, and some of them had little clue as to what was going on.

The Armed Forces works on paperwork even now, in triplicate, usually (or duplicate, at least). You basically had to fill in form after form to draw stores, clothing, transport, and even to eat; some of the recruits fell well below standard with form compilation, and you would help them out without ridicule. One of my closest early friends came from Manchester and could not even write his name at that time. He was illiterate, and embarrassingly, it still happens now, with education standards well below that expected. However, my life-long friend was terrific at the assault course, and you would tag along with him when you needed a lift over the wall, so helping him fill out a form seemed a small price to pay.

You did that to get through, to survive, to progress to that next week and another challenge. That 'can do' attitude is instilled in you; you help your colleagues, and that is something you never lose.

Problem solving and teamwork are everything, and by far the hardest test of New Entry training was probably the most ironic. I could not swim with heavy clothing on and failed by a small margin on several tests. I could swim but struggled, and no pass meant a very quick end to my service career; I was out.

I went down to the pool with every spare minute I had,

and I did not have many of them. One of the boys helped me, and within three months, I was on the swimming team. It was all about technique; they helped me with my technique, and PNST was adorned on my service record (four letters which stood for 'Passed Naval Swimming Test'). It was one of the hardest things that I have achieved to gain those four letters on a piece of paper; the water does not care how clever you are. After all the years I was in submarines, I question how much use the PNST would be if I had to get out in an emergency.

I sat amongst the group, and whilst my childhood was far from conventional, I realised that my dad and grandparents had done an excellent job. I was ahead of most people at most things; all those nights being angry doing things for my grandparents or my dad's business had paid off.

Certainly, achieving practical tasks, having confidence, and showing emotional strength were all strong in me, and I could handle setbacks better than others. I had been through a few personal disasters, whereas some other guys had never experienced much in life.

I was confident enough to ask for help. Other boys would clam up and not do that, and they would end up walking. But I did not want to go home and say that I had failed. I was fiercely proud of where I came from (and still am) but more importantly what I was to become.

Six weeks was a long time, and people dropped out every day, loads of them. Sadly, it would be people I had got on with, but they decided they had been broken, and enough was enough. Looking back now, we did some strange things in terms of being in the Navy, long cross-country runs and assault courses, but they were designed to test you and push you to the breaking point.

Those six weeks were particularly important in my career; it was my first time at being away on my own. I was isolated and had no one to talk to within my family. The chief petty officer would say, 'I am your mum and dad now,' and you could confide in him, to some extent. They were hard people, especially during the day, but in quiet moments late into the evening, over a cup of tea and a bit of cake, they were alright.

However, greater dangers were ahead, and after only three days in uniform, I had to call and tell my grandparents the Royal Navy had given me a gun.

We went to qualify with live ammo at the small arms firing range and were told nobody could fail, as we would be guarding the Naval Base at the weekend. You would fear the dark, and they gave you a rifle with six rounds of ammunition; I was walking around like Corporal Jones from *Dad's Army*. All I could think of repeatedly was the fact that what if there were seven intruders? I would probably miss with my first shot and fire the other five, chuck the gun away, and run. You think strange things like that when you are on your own as a sixteen-year-old kid with a gun; it was a bloody long couple of hours guarding the local oil tanks, but I took great delight in telling my folks about my very important part in defending the British Empire.

Then it was over, six weeks had gone, 'Passed Part 1 Training' was duly scribed on my service record, and a proud day receiving not just a certificate for the best student from the quirkily named Captain Gerkin, RN, but more important to me, a hug from a proud father.

I was not sure of the future but Part 2 Communications Training at nearby HMS Mercury, Petersfield in Hampshire, beckoned and another small step towards a thirty-four-year love affair with submarines, but first there was the prospect of two weeks' advance of pay and more importantly fourteen days' leave. Yep, the Royal Navy was always going to be an excellent career choice.

OUT ON MY OWN

Being on leave in Surfleet was suddenly strangely difficult. The fact that you are away from home and friends means you return after a few weeks out of tune with what is going on. The late 1970s was a changing time, with unemployment rising, wages falling, and fewer traditional seasonal jobs due to increased mechanisation. After a few days, I became bored and longed to get back to Mercury and my next challenge. I had changed; gone was my fear and insecurity, replaced by confidence and at times a brash attitude. I needed to get back to the path I had chosen, and as things were now on an even plane at Surfleet, the two weeks' leave were dragging in the extreme.

Communications training was by far the longest course, being some five months long, and as a result, we considered ourselves a cut above the rest; the basics like Morse code came naturally to me, and an above class average of eighteen words per minute did not go unnoticed by my superiors. Morse was still used extensively in the submarine service mainly due to the other NATO nations lagging with technology. My only fear was that if I volunteered, as I had to, being under eighteen, I would face more training at the RN Submarine School at nearby HMS Dolphin at Gosport and the intimidating Submarine Escape Tank Trainer (SETT) with its hundred metres of water to negotiate. This all seemed daunting to a person who only a few weeks past had floundered in the swimming pool at HMS Raleigh. Advice came from a friendly corner, my instructor, Radio Supervisor Dutchy Holland, who knew all about submarines, having served on diesel electric boats (as that's what they are called) for eons, and unlike picking winning horses, his daily passion, he knew the ins and outs of being a sun dodger. His response was instant

'Son, I've seen more wasters here over the years who didn't see the opportunities on offer; submariners are a breed apart, and to wear a qualified submariner's badge is respected, whoever you are and whatever you are.'

Dutchy was a good instructor and sound person to boot, and although he had a hard exterior, he was respected by all at Mercury, and I had no reason to doubt him. My mind was set; signing to transfer to the submarine service also added an additional fourteen weeks to training and, more importantly, more weekends when off duty at my beloved Highbrook to see my ailing grandmother. The Friday routine was always the same for a weekend at Highbrook: You lined up in full uniform in the drill shed to get paid in the hand with hard cash, and woe betide if you were not dressed smartly or showed disrespect by not saluting the paymaster. Each pay parade I received seventeen pounds in the hand, followed by a train journey from Petersfield to Haywards Heath to be picked up by my grandfather, followed up with an omelette and chips, lovingly prepared. I can remember the first time going home in uniform, and my usually diminutive grandmother was taller than a giant with pride. It made me feel good, as it was obvious she was struggling and in deep pain. My grandfather did not outwardly show any real concern, but inside, I knew he was in turmoil; time was fast ebbing away for the strongest partnership I knew. Even a couple of drinks in the nearby British Legion Club at Danehill would not make his guard slip; he did not want anyone to fuss, typically laidback Grandad.

I loved being in his company, and Bill was loved by everyone he encountered. During World War II, he had seen reserved occupation as a farmer in the Slough/Langley area and had manned the guns during air raids as part of the local Home Guard unit; his unit claimed a kill of a German bomber one dark night in 1940 but with no subsequent wreckage found to substantiate it. The claim became stark reality in the 1960s when the extensive Langley ponds were dredged to reveal a very well-preserved Dornier bomber with a less-than-preserved crew still strapped in. The outcome and identity I have never investigated, but I'd like to think it is a simple lifelong lesson of never piss around with the Ford family.

LIFE IN A BLUE SUIT

The second of August 1977 became the pivotal point of a life in uniform, and the thirty-four years to follow were a heady mix of conflict, joy, love, passion, gains, and losses, and like a *Star Wars* film (probably for a later book, if spared), as most of the period was spent with the Cold War very much to the fore. I remember vividly when the Falklands conflict happened; we were really caught out in the intelligence world, where all our linguists save for a few unlucky people dispatched eight thousand miles south with some speed; all learnt and spoke Russian. The period all spent in numerous submarines was a time of immense belonging for the boy from Sussex and lifelong friendships and camaraderie to this day. We try and meet up each year, and the stories of days past get more and more twisted, but the only thing consistent is a bond which can never be explained, unless you are a submariner. Taking a bullet for a comrade is an old saying, but it is still there as we get older, not any wiser, and I know will prevail until our maker calls us.

Like any occupation which involves separation from family, in 1990, I was divorced from first wife Kerry and drew up a unique situation; having decided to move away from Plymouth and home in nearby Cornwall, I volunteered for any Portsmouth-based submarine, to which an obviously witty drafting officer assigned me to the Portsmouth-based diesel electric submarine HMS *Opossum,* in refit, in Plymouth. I am indebted to two commanding officers of the *Opossum,* namely Tom Herman and Steve Upright, for giving me the opportunity in 1994 to attend the Admiralty Interview Board, where I was duly selected to become a commissioned officer in the Royal Navy. Passing out at a royal parade at the Britannic Royal Naval College at Dartmouth, Devon, was a red-letter day, with my father again standing tall, and I am sure others were looking down with pride. *Opossum* was without doubt another turning point in a career and life at sea. In 1990/91, the *Opossum* conducted a world tour, which was interrupted on the return leg by service in the Gulf War.

I was met by my family after an eleven-month deployment away from home; this was another great day but tinged with sadness, as the submarine home in Gosport, Hampshire, HMS *Dolphin* was too close to operational vessels and the start of the end for diesel electric submarines in the Royal Navy (a mistake to me and most people and a loss of unique skills from a branch of the submarine service unlikely to return). Operating diesel electric submarines requires special qualities, and sadly those are dying as friends cross the bar (Naval slang for dying). Submariners are a tight-knit bunch, but those who serve in diesel electrics were closer to the edge, dangerwise, and the consequences of getting things wrong were much higher. That having been said, living life on the edge was much more fun and drew a crew together.

The Cold War has largely been forgotten, but it was a serious period of our history, and the sacrifice of the Armed Forces has never been formally recognised. There have been calls for a Cold War medal to be awarded to those who served, but as in most cases, the moment has passed, and the greatest recognition is that bond between the aging veterans. The explosion of social media has been good for those of us left to tell a tale or two and share it with a wider audience, who may think such stories too extreme to be true, but never underestimate the old boy sat in the corner of some bar, nursing a beer, deep in thought and maybe with a tear in his eye. Thirty-four years' service to any employer is something to be rightly proud of; people are always asking if I miss my life in submarines, but it's the people you miss and the way of life, life meaning life.

The limitations of the Official Secrets Act mean I can say little about this period of my life, but I remain proud of my service and of all the recognition over the period, I deem my Long Service and Good Conduct medal as the highest honour. Loyalty is a word used far too often and not endorsed by actions, and when asked about what I consider to be my biggest strength, it's simply that; in work or to the people you grow up with and love and laugh with, it counts for everything. With three serious personal relationships in my life crumbling, I can honestly say that I maintained that stance well into the postrecovery stage, which is painful in the extreme, but that's what I perceive to be right and a value my grandparents diligently instilled. As the years go by, you invariably lose people from your working days, and often the latest reunion is often a funeral, but surreally often again, laughter can be heard as an old story is remembered and the bounds of impossibility totally irrelevant. The submarine community is not a large one, and everyone knows everyone just about from a certain era, and the loss of anyone is felt deeply. Bonds in the military are always strong in the extreme, but I defy anyone to show me a group closer-knit than submariners.

LIFE CHANGES; SURVIVING THE CRISIS

I was lucky to serve in the great naval ports of Portsmouth and Plymouth, but inevitably, the modern home of the submarine is Helensburgh on the River Clyde, and the submarine base of nearby Faslane in Scotland became homeport.

Newly diagnosed with Parkinson's in 2011, I needed to snap out of my sense of ineptitude, and I immersed myself totally in the day-to-day running of my local football team East Stirlingshire, the Mighty Shire. Without doubt, this decision was to stop me taking my own life, as depression and at times anger had set in to such a state, my whole demeanour had changed, and even my personal standards were becoming strained. I had always loved football, and my earliest memories apart from 1966 and 'They think it's all over' were centred around my father and friends, who every other Saturday would clamber into the smallest of cars, with myself wedged in the back, and set off via the pub to watch Brighton and Hove Albion, a club I still follow to this day.

The Sloop Inn was a favourite prematch watering hole, and for an hour, I would be subjected to sitting in the back seat of the car with a bottle of cola whilst the lads had a few pints before, piling back in the car and driving off to the holy grail of the Goldstone Ground, Hove. Things did not always go to plan at the game, with Brighton as perennial strugglers in the 1970s, and things did not always go smoothly with the transport, either, with the car catching fire one day and flooded at the pub after heavy rain caused the nearby river to inundate the car park. On both occasions, I was stuck on the back seat but somehow lived to tell the tale. Such is the drama of supporting or running any club, and East Stirlingshire in Falkirk, Scotland, was to be my salvation.

The trials and tribulations of East Stirlingshire Football Club are well documented, and my first instinct was to not put pen to paper about the club in any big way, but people would wonder why not, and in hindsight, it has been a major part in my rehabilitation and, in some areas, my personal downfall that I let it rule my life for so many years. Association football is an international passion, a language, a way of life and a pressure release valve for so many, but different words can be used when you are battling to keep a small club afloat. Anyone who daily struggles to run any club on a shoestring has my respects but the Shire could not even afford a shoestring when I was asked to get involved.

It used to amaze me why anyone being of sound mind and body would ever get involved with a football club, apart from turning up on a match day to shout for often meaningless reasons at people running around with a ball. Of course, as a young lad, everyone wanted to be a footballer, and I grew up with the likes of the late, great George Best, who I had the honour to see play in the flesh, but strangely, my idols were varied. I guess my interest in football was wholesale and not just a local team. I am unashamedly a

Brighton and Hove Albion fan to this day and have been since sitting atop my father's shoulders as a kid at the old Goldstone Ground in Hove. I suppose through thick and thin, the Seagulls have survived, but the game in Scotland is a totally different ball game.

My love affair with my latest local club started pretty much by accident; at the time, in 1995, I was serving on a nuclear-powered submarine, HMS *Renown,* in Faslane, on the west coast of Scotland, at the Clyde Submarine Base. As officer of the day (OOD), the weekend duty watch on the boat (that is what submarines are traditionally called) was normally split with two officers, one doing Friday and Sunday and the other the Saturday. I particularly liked the Friday/Sunday as it meant a seriously lazy day on the Saturday, with a chance to do the washing, read all the newspapers, drink coffee, have a beer in the almost deserted bar on the evening, and most of all catch up on sleep. The Friday night duty this particular week had been a long one, as the majority of the crew were dispatched on leave for two weeks, and as usual, the majority of routine tasks were delegated to the overnight duty watch, which in itself was nothing I disliked, as it helped pass the time, but invariably it meant little or no sleep.

All submarine operations alongside have an element of danger and consequence if you get it wrong, and permission was always sought from the OOD; it mattered not if it was 3 a.m. Such is the responsibility of the safety and responsibility delegated to the OOD from the commanding officer whilst he is away from the submarine, a nuclear submarine at that with a powerful reactor; *Renown* was a Polaris submarine, so the safety of embarked missiles doubly focussed the mind.

It feels great to walk off the boat in the morning having handed over the charge of one of Her Majesty's modern-day battleships, and the slow amble up to the officers' wardroom to a full cooked breakfast is in my top ten. That fateful day, it was to be a little different, as upon entering the wardroom, I was confronted by what can only be described as a shell of a human being.

Iain Rae, a fellow *Renownie* and no-nonsense Scot, had obviously, instead of travelling the thirty-odd miles to his folks' house on the Friday night, decided to have a few beers in nearby Helensburgh, and as was often the case, the thirty-odd miles was beyond the navigational skills of Iain, and two quid in a taxi back to base was an easier option. Iain had almost made it to his room, but the settees in the main foyer of the wardroom was as far as his legs could manage. It seemed only right to kick his arse and get him to join me at breakfast. Iain had a medical background but had decided to become a seaman officer, and for someone with such medical knowledge, he knew how to push his body to the limit. Drinking, smoking, and a large fried brekkie was taken in his stride, and within an hour, Iain was looking for more.

The suggestion was made that I should join him for drinks at his folks' and also to take in the local football derby game that afternoon, but all I could see was being lumbered with having to provide a free taxi for Iain to somewhere called Stenhousemuir, and in the days before satnavs in cars, I hadn't a bloody clue where that was, and the chances of Iain knowing even less. I decided to decline the offer and headed for my room. No sleep and a double-sized breakfast soon had the desired effect, and sleep came easily, but only for a short moment in time, as although I had locked my door, Iain had clambered in the bloody window (even though I was on the second floor) and decided to make me an offer I just couldn't refuse: his words, not mine.

Having a near twenty-stone hungover jock perched on the end of your bed was something I decided was not worth living for, so the road trip to the promised land, or Stenny, as home for Iain was affectionately known, was laid out before us. The plan was simple: We drive to Stenny, have beer, watch football, have beer, back to Iain's folks for tea and drink beer, go out on the town and drink beer, and if we don't get lucky, back to Iain's for a late beer. My overriding concern was twofold, in that I had to get back to base for the 0900 changeover the next morning and to be in a fit state to carry out my duty. The requirement in those distant days was no alcohol eight hours before duty, but I was acutely aware that even at that point, I would be bloody useless the next day, and to confound the problem, Iain's brother Clive was joining us on our adventure. Clive made Iain look like a novice when it came to drink.

So that is where it is.

Fully booted and spurred, the trip to the People's Republic of Stenhousemuir was particularly pleasant. The central belt of Scotland has its down points, but the journey along the A811 to Stirling is a great route to see the real Scotland, and by the time of turning on to the M9 motorway and leaving the imposing Stirling Castle in our wake, I was actually buzzing and thinking maybe giving up my lazy Saturday was not such a bad idea, after all; Iain had even stayed awake to keep us on track (something I do to this day is to keep a mental note of landmarks for the return journey, as more than not, it would be dark and raining for sure; this was Scotland, after all).

How can you describe Stenny? You would need a great deal of postcards for starters, and a sense of humour would probably not go amiss. Perched on the outskirts of industrial Falkirk, Stenny had nothing but numerous pubs and the sense of 'It will be okay when it's finished,' but the promised land had one jewel in its crown and the total devotion of the Rae family: the football club Stenhousemuir FC, the Warriors. It was only after a couple of prematch beers that I asked who the mighty Warriors were playing that day, and the response was muttered, 'The bloody Shire.' The bloody Shire, or to give them their proper name, East Stirlingshire Football and Athletic Club, were from the centre of Falkirk, and with Falkirk FC themselves made up the fact that Falkirk had three senior football teams, one to remember for any pub quiz night. Not quite the Old Firm, City, and United in Manchester, but nonetheless important for bragging rights on a Monday morning, the Shire/Stenny local derby was the big one to the five hundred or so souls who supported the two teams.

Sitting in a bar without a single window and a surprisingly decent beer, I suddenly realised that the place was devoid of Shire supporters, which was quickly explained to me that on a local match day, the Shire fans basically walked the few miles from central Falkirk to Stenhousemuir, but with a twist. To a Shire fan, the Stenny Walk involved walking to the match at Ochilview and stopping in each pub for a drink as they meandered and increasingly staggered towards the game. To this day, I am still unsure exactly how many pubs the route entails, save to say it is a bloody lot, even if you are only having a swift half in each. By the time three o'clock arrived, the wee ground was surprisingly buzzing with a decent support from both clubs, but with the Shire faithful certainly the noisier, no doubt fuelled up by the local public houses.

It was at this point my own consumption began to tell, and I made a decision which was to have wide-ranging implications: to defect to the dark side and join the Shire supporters. I was hooked, and the love affair with East Stirlingshire Football and Athletic Club began, and through thick and thin (mainly thin, it must be said), I am Shire till I die. I cannot even remember the score line, but it was a Shire win, and of course the obligatory celebration was to continue well into the night and even later into the Sunday morning, and I realised that I had to be back on base for 9 a.m., which was going to be difficult with no mobile phones and satnavs in those distant days.

Like a one-legged homing pigeon, I made it back to base in surprisingly good order, the only danger the suicidal rabbits and crows on the A811 Stirling straights, a seriously good road for trying to break the land speed record, and a dangerous road during busy periods, but on a Sunday morning it was good to go!

Shire's own ground was situated to the rear of a carpet retail shop off the main shopping area known as Central Retail Park in Falkirk town centre; affectionately known as Firs Park, it was best described as quirky and basically lacked everything including grass for long periods each season. That said, it had something special about it; maybe simply the loyal supporters or the lack of amenities like toilets that had a flushing system that flushed without the aid of a bucket. I remember a Gretna fan saying that Firs Park was a 'fucking shithole', but it was *our* fucking shithole, and the best was made of a bad thing as football at this level in Scotland was basically like the gents' toilet: a busted flush.

The one thing the club had, though, was a history, a history which can brag that Sir Alec Ferguson had managed the team as his first job in a long and illustrious career, not shared at East Stirlingshire with the only success of note beating the local big club Falkirk in a local cup game. Everyone associated with the club, it seemed, was a character, and the chairman/secretary was no different. Les Thomson had been a good player himself in the past locally and then in his late sixties had found himself the ultimate impossible employment as the custodian of a club in major debt and a bleak future.

The club had been formed in 1880 in nearby Bainsford, and the successes over the years had been rare. Save to say it was still afloat (just) after all those years and largely down to Les, who had been the proverbial plate spinner. Les was openly despised by many supporters for his frugal manner in running a senior club such as the Shire, but the truth was black and white, like the home shirts: The club had no money, and in fact, it was far worse, in that the club owed so much, it was guilty of trading in the red. Les must be given credit in keeping it afloat through impossible means, it seemed, at times. I remember meeting Les for the very first time in his office, a small room at the end of the narrow corridor at Firs Park. It was less of an office and more of a chaotic mixture of books, kit, paperwork, club trophies (yes, it's true), the odd bottle of booze, and a battered photocopier in the corner. Les sat at the end behind an equally chaotic desk dominated by a battered club tea mug and an in tray of largely final demand bills and letters from the Scottish Football Association demanding club compliance and complaints.

Always immaculately dressed, Les would defend the club with vigour from all and sundry, and over the years had developed a rhino-like skin, impervious to fatal blows. I think Les sometimes even took pleasure in getting away with things, especially the likes of the SFA based at the national stadium Hampden Park in Glasgow, and the charm was always switched on when talking to the female staff therein—un-PC, naturally; he would often call any woman 'Toots', much to the amusement of us all.

I was always astounded by Les's popularity when I later attended league meetings at Hampden as a club director. Other chairman always clamoured to sit with Les at lunch, and there was always not so much sympathy but love for the affable man who at times could have turned the bottled water into wine; let's face it, many other clubs were in a similar battle to find cash and to keep going. Such was the state of the game in Scotland, and to this day, it remains the biggest issue. I remember the advice (or should I say briefing) by Les prior to my first ever meeting with him at Hampden: 'Grab us some seats at the back where we are safest in case things get sticky and we are delayed for lunch. You are quicker than any of these miserable sods and leap away and grab the attention of the serving staff.'

Les was the master of the freebie and getting something for nothing. Years of running the club on a shoestring would mean even the league meeting complimentary pens would end up in his bag, and I recall the fits of laughter once in the car home when he revealed he had swiped the pen off the Falkirk chairman, who had stood up to address the floor and having sat back down again had to ask Les to borrow his pen.

Les could also be infuriating, and I had cause to have words with him over the payment of bills. He would wait until the very last minute to pay any bill but the dues owed to the electricity company. The club needed lights on a match day pretty much most of the time, and that would be a tad difficult without any power. It was probably a bonus when the lights went out in the gents' toilet, but matches had to be played. The first act on becoming a director at the club was to pay personally for the electric bill and the small matter of buying some light bulbs, which left the home fans in wonderment, as they could suddenly see the horror on display each week. There is a standard of lux measurement of floodlights, and somehow, the beaks at Hampden never seemed to catch us out. Such was the persuasiveness of Les in getting past regulations, although the streetlights in the nearby road were at times doing more for the club than the dead bulbs around the pitch.

Football is addictive; trust me, I know, and it cost me, financially and personally. The wave of success (or not) was not measured by the result on a Saturday, but by the mere fact we had enough money or cash in the tin to pay the bills and go for another week. It has been well documented that many players were paid the princely sum of ten pounds a week, which did not even cover the costs of personal travel to training twice a week and to a match day.

As chief exec, secretary, safety officer, caterer, and anything else required of him, Les was only one of two people employed full-time by the club, the other being Jimmy Wilson, the groundsman and kit man. Jimmy became a great friend, along with his assistant and stalwart Robert Jack; they were the soul of the club and, along with Les, exponents of the freebie. Having become a regular helper around the club in the late 1990s, I soon realised that the only way the club had survived was by simple loyalty, which extended to the supporters who week in and week out turned up to watch much endeavour but very little success on the field of play. Everyone loves an underdog, unless you are that underdog, and finishing bottom of the Scottish Football League (SFL) each season became normality; there were times when you left the ground after a battering on a Saturday wondering why you bothered, but then the friendly face of a supporter would quip, 'See you next week, Fordy; they can't be that bad again, surely?'

The fact was, they probably would be worse, but just occasionally, a small positive would give renewed hope, and somebody else had to read the Sunday newspaper, having been dumped by the worst team in Britain. The weight of history was also something I was acutely aware of, a club born in 1880, and although in terminal decline, some might say I could never have been the one to see the door close on history, and inadvertently, the need to preserve the club as a going concern consumed me. It was easy to just put my hand in my pocket and pay for things, albeit sometimes small, and a packet of toilet rolls for match day could be just as important as a new match ball.

The state of the Firs Park's grounds was a constant worry, and I remember asking Jimmy what was needed to sort out the issues, and after ten minutes, I wished I had not bothered. For a start, the physical dimensions of the pitch did not reach the required standard as set out by the Scottish Football Association, and thus far, Les had weaved his influence and charm in getting the club a waiver, but post-Hillsborough, even this far down the football structure meant things had to change. The pitch was a couple of metres shorter than that required, but it might have been any distance; it mattered little, as Firs Park was hemmed in on all sides by development. It simply did not measure up and never would. The pitch itself for a period in late July to early August looked fantastic with lush green grass and, lovingly prepared by Jimmy and Robert, would look the part with the pitch marked out for the first home game.

The trouble was the pitch grass was soil based, and although immaculate early season, the Scottish winter weather would soon leave the grass in a poor state, and mud rather than grass would soon be the norm. Jimmy and Robert worked wonders with a lawn mower more suited to an agricultural museum and without the resources to top dress the pitch to prolong its usefulness. The other factor was the mere fact that the ground at Firs Park was used not just for a match day but also doubled up as a training venue each and every Tuesday and Thursday, such was the need with no funding for a separate facility for training. A postponed game on a Saturday with an unplayable pitch was a disaster in the dark days of the 1990s, as without that match income, the bills still had to be paid the following week.

I remember Les just about pleading with the referee on numerous occasions simply to get the game played, and with strict guidelines about rolling balls and lines being visible, even on mud, it was a fraught time. But somehow the club survived, and seeing first-hand the wheeling and dealing day to day by Les must have led to sleepless nights; the critics on the terraces would often give some verbal stick to him, but later as chairman of the club, I looked back and wondered how the hell the plate-spinning worked. Although at times infuriating, Les deserved great credit.

I do recall a week in the late 1990s when due to work commitments, injuries, and suspensions, the manager was struggling to put a team on the pitch for an important match with Shire, the proverbial six-pointer. It was obvious on the Thursday of that week that the weather was not going to help the club's cause, with sunshine and record-breaking warm temperatures forecast. I remember calling Jimmy on the Friday afternoon from my home in Dunblane to check what was needed for the Saturday, to be told by him that the game was off due to a waterlogged pitch. It soon became evident that although the whole of the UK was basking in wall-to-wall sunshine, a cloudburst had occurred in Falkirk around Firs Street, leading to wholesale flooding.

I quickly rang Les, who confirmed the local referee had been called in and had deemed the pitch unplayable. It soon became evident that this timely act of God was in fact an act of Blue Watch at the local fire station and the overzealous testing of hydrants in and around the ground, instigated by two members of the ground staff and aided by several cases of ale as currency.

Every football club will tell you quite simply they have the best fans, and I have often wondered how that should be measured. The bigger clubs will point to the number of season tickets sold, and others would point to the amount of revenue generated, but there is only one measurement in my opinion, and that's the sheer belief someone has in an impossible situation but is still willing to be involved. In 2011, the two hundred or so hard-core fans of East Stirlingshire founded Shiretrust, the revolutionary route of club ownership by a supporter's trust, and the football trust revolution is still happening today, trying to remove bad ownership by people or organisations bent on asset stripping for self-gain.

I had seen it first-hand, as Brighton and Hove Albion Football Club had been just about deemed extinct by debt and poor ownership in the 1980s, and the fans, with some clever direct action, pulled it finally together, and I suppose an example which has seen the club prosper, with supporters in key positions within the club. In 2010, the Shire had such a low fan base, many even in the Scottish game saw the demise of the club as a mercy killing, but to those two hundred, it had been a tradition of going to the match week in and week out. Father and son had given way to whole families being connected to the club through blind loyalty, and I personally tried to contribute as best I could, despite having a full-time job prior to my Parkinson's diagnosis in 2011.

The club was continually on death row, it seemed, but credit must be given to those who saw the dedication of the fans; they put money and time into the club to keep it afloat, albeit mostly short-term, but survive it has to this day. I have so many friends still at East Stirlingshire, and each has the club at heart; to single out individuals would be wrong, but the investment by Spencer Fearn, a Yorkshire-based businessman, allowed the club to operate with supporters at the heart of the business, which football really is and a fact people readily ignore. Spencer remains a good friend and, of course, a Shire supporter, but first and foremost a successful businessman, and to be successful, you do not invest long term in Scottish football.

Spencer's buying up of club shares in 2010 led the way in transferring the club to near supporter control in 2011, and hard decisions made to ground share and use alternative facilities for training. The message was clear in that you may be small, but you can still be professional. I still use that model and remember getting a call from a commercial manager from a Scottish Premier club, asking what we were doing new, as Hampden had told him the Shire are 'doing good things.'

I would sit at meetings with Les, surrounded by the chairman, financial director, and so on from the bigger clubs and listen to the unsustainable plans of just about all of them, who believed that a loan from a bank was good business and would demand more and more money to simply spend on paying players with the fear of going out of business forced to the back of the mind, akin to an ostrich with its head in the sand.

JUST A POUND

I'm not quite sure how it happened to this day, but there was a Shiretrust meeting around late summer 2011, and the news was out that the football club was to finally be owned and controlled by supporters. Les Thomson had been offered Spencer's shares for a pound, a pound I had to lend him the year before, and now Les was to resign completely from the football club, a shock personally, but Les was not well, and the pressure of football administration had taken its toll. It is bad enough running a football club with funds and personnel, but to do everything with an overdraft is the reason for sleepless nights. About overdrafts: Les had somehow convinced the bank to extend ours to twenty thousand pounds, and that was used to the limit; at times, I wondered if Les understood the context of having to pay it back at some avenue.

The club's bank manager was a regular visitor to the ground, not to buy a replica team shirt or scarf but purely to check the club was trading in the black, and it really was hand to mouth. Going to the bank with Les was an education and always a pleasure and sometimes became a bit of a staff outing, as the large metal door at Firs Park would be firmly slammed shut and locked, for what reason became less obvious, as nothing really was worth stealing. Les would slip into the bank with Robert and Jimmy in tow to chat up the nervous female staff, whilst I was left to deal with the cashier, not so pleased having to count a load of change.

In truth, the joy of being a small but lovable team appealed to me immensely, and all three of the Musketeers were great company; at times, when the pressure was off, the scrapes and adventures would eclipse anything else I have experienced in my football years. After the bank, there was round two of chatting up the staff in the nearby Tesco store on the retail park adjacent to the ground, and the coffees would always need a 'wee cake'; the slow walk across the car park to the aging Firs would be full of laughs and banter, with Jimmy probably the brunt of most of it, but he loved being the star.

Jimmy was a great friend and always had a kind word for you; things never fazed him, the classic man with can-do skills. My overriding image of Jimmy is a figure constantly moaning about footballers, the weather, the fucking grass, the arseholes who blocked the toilets, no fags for Christ's sake, and the game is off, but wherever we went, Jimmy and Robert would be the centre of attention, respected as football men and above all else as close friends. Sadly, Jimmy died on my wedding day to Kate (my second wife). It was also Scottish Cup Final Day, with Falkirk in the final versus Rangers, but Robert and Les only broke the news after I was married. In hindsight, my loss that day was twofold, but the sun shone, and a glass was raised to the best groundsman ever to grace the game, but most of all my friend. 'There's only one Jimmy Wilson' rang out at the next home game after the summer break, and I remember Robert's eulogy at the funeral; his last words were, 'Have a good season, pal.'

I for one will never forget my wedding anniversary.

Firs Park was also the subject of a tug of war between the supporters and the actual owner, a previous chairman, Alan Mackin, who was openly despised by all and sundry (and is still). Alan had made no secret of the fact that his intention was to sell the ground for redevelopment for personal gain, but to this day, the ground remains overgrown and demolished behind the big steel door, which still protects the fact that there is bugger all worth stealing still. The only act of theft I can recall was an attempt by a local lad who decided one night to steal the goal posts for scrap. The flaw to this criminal mastermind's plan was the sheer weight of the said items, which were steel and not aluminium, and in attempting to navigate his way out of the ground with the crossbar, akin to the Keystone Kops, he became overbalanced and was apprehended by the local Falkirk constabulary and charged with theft.

Inadvertently, this individual's act helped the club financially, in that the media loved to have a go at the Shire, basically the United Kingdom's worst professional club. Sympathy led to a sponsorship opportunity with Littlewoods Pools, and although results did not really improve on the pitch, the playing kit with the club's new sponsor's logo became a firm favourite and sold well. Les never really divulged just how much we received from Littlewoods, and the clubs accounts were the biggest work of fiction since Enid Blyton decided to put pen to paper, but it was a welcome boost nonetheless.

A past club manager, Jim McInally, summed up the

lure of football ambition, often misguided, in that there is always someone who thinks they are the person to bring success to even the downtrodden of clubs such as the Shire. There are only a finite number of opportunities in the game in Scotland, and I can remember some of the high-profile applicants for the vacant manager's or head coach's roles at the club over the years. Some simply got the job as they wanted no pay, just the opportunity to manage a team, albeit a team of extremely limited ability. When I first got involved with Les, I can remember the current manager Dennis Newall had simply impressed Les by saying he would do the job for free. Dennis was not blessed with success and had the misfortune of being sacked by Alan Mackin via a text message from Spain and being informed his contract was being cancelled, which would have been fine if a contract had existed.

The shambles at the club during the 1990s and into the early 2000s knew no bounds, and something had to give. The introduction of supporters on the club board was a massive coup, and the mere fact that Chairman Alan Mackin was spending all his time in Spain and leaving Les with the task of survival meant the trust could make slow but steady inroads into the running of the club. The 2003–2004 season had been a total disaster, with the team only gaining a meagre eight points, a record low for any UK senior club, and it became all hands to the pump; although there was no relegation from the Scottish League, the football beaks at Hampden were coming under real pressure to introduce relegation, and the Shire's demise, for sure.

Shiretrust became the focus of the real supporters and attracted casual football fans from around the world as well as the local faithful with fundraising allowing direct help to the club's day-to-day running. The first beneficiaries were Robert and Jimmy, who took delivery of a brand-spanking-new mower to try and allow the pitch some long overdue love and attention. I can clearly remember the morning that the three-thousand-pound-plus beast turned up. I had managed to convince a local supplier that the club had great media contacts and to be associated with the club would bring them great benefit (I simply left out the fact that the media attention was largely derogatory in the extreme). I recall the joy of seeing Jimmy with the look of an expectant father awaiting a new child and the unadulterated pleasure when the Ransome 24 cylinder kissed the hallowed turf of Firs Park.

The mower even had a seat, but this was a trick too far for Jimmy, who preferred to trudge behind in his wellies with cigarette dangling from his lips and carefully running up and down the pitch. Robert was more pragmatic and used the ride on, which also incorporated a second roller, and the pride of a pitch immaculately cut with lines sweeping from one end to the other caused a wow from supporters, who had for years seen grass mostly gnawed than cut.

The club has had (and continues to have) some colourful supporters on the terraces, and the introduction of the trust's inclusion led many to assist in the mundane jobs such as weeding around the pitch and the unenviable job of painting the gents' toilets. Although a renewed sense of optimism abounded, the stark reality was that on the park, the players were still struggling to gain results, and 2007 had seen the club finish bottom of the Scottish 3rd Division for the fifth season in a row, a fact not missed by the Scottish Football League.

Wednesday, 2 May 2007, was an education I will never forget and without doubt Les Thomson's finest hour. On finishing bottom, the club had been summoned to HQ at Hampden to explain why we had finished last yet again. In short, we were basically crap on the park, and on the way to Glasgow, I remember Les saying, 'What else can I say? It's bloody obvious.'

The usual sense of foreboding engulfed me as we trudged up the steps to the front door and not helped by the heavy rain, which always seemed to be the norm when we were in trouble with the top table. Les swept onto the top floor and instantly was on the offensive. We were seated in front of the full committee, and Les pulled the trump card out of his pocket. Spencer Fearn had told Les in some secrecy that he was to invest forty thousand pounds in the club, a major shot in the arm for any club, let alone the Shire. Spencer had also outlined his desire to see youth teams reintroduced after being disbanded as a cost-cutting measure, as well as paying wages to attract better players.

It had been no secret to the committee that the club had underpaid the players for several seasons, and I passionately believed this was a big pointer on the day to a positive outcome. All penalties were on the table that day for the club to finish bottom the following season. Expulsion was ultimate but in the short term, the club could have lost its status as a member club and would therefore receive no further central league funding, a death knell for sure for the club founded in 1880.

Spencer had been appointed to the board of club

directors and had ambitions to see the club owned outright, which was to become a major battle with Chairman Alan Mackin, a battle to become increasingly brutal over the following weeks. The biggest news was that the club had reached an outline agreement to groundshare with local rivals Stenhousemuir, with the costs of upgrading Firs Park outweighing the cost of sharing. I make no apologies for saying I was disappointed at not looking at other possibilities for match days. Although the deal to share at Ochilview Park was costly, it had the appeal of being ready in all respects for match day standards. The Shire would have access to a ready-made facility, and for the first time in years, any shortfalls in standards would need to be addressed by Stenhousemuir.

As ever, the details of any groundshare deal were complex and at times extremely tiresome, and underlying everything was a need to find the cash to pay for it still. The concerns of the league committee that day were long and drawn out, but the masterclass by Les in battling against the odds was a joy to behold. I passionately believe that nobody apart from Les had the respect of the ordinary football people in that room, but he pulled it off and did with aplomb. I fully expected the worse, but the sympathy and common sense in the room that day was heartfelt, and we escaped with basically a decree not to finish bottom the following season and a list of sanctions if we did.

As ever, Les had pulled it off, and as ever, he never got the credit he deserved from many supporters, who saw it more as a sell-out, especially having to face the prospect of playing along the road in Stenny. The biggest grievance was down purely to cash and the club basically bankrolling their arch-rivals, but time was against us, and the deal was done. Spencer came in, and a will to succeed was forcibly instilled, with the club having a full-time commercial manager for the first time I could remember; the visits by the bank manager also stopped, again for the first time in my memory. Experienced managers and coaches started to attract better players to the club, and training took on a whole new professional style and purpose, but it was still going to be tough after years of mediocrity.

The agreement to hire Ochilview (for that is what it was, simply a pay-to-play deal and not ground sharing) became a major challenge for each home game. Personally, I did not even like using the word 'Home', but decanting the club the few miles along the road became a well-oiled process. Playing kit, club shop items, programmes, and even boardroom hospitality drinks and food made its way along the Bainsford Road, and after the game, back it all came. Under the agreement, we were obliged to use the catering facilities supplied by Stenhousemuir, and at first, many of the East Stirlingshire support boycotted the well-stocked pie hut on the main stand concourse, but with winter fixtures and a dip in temperature, the need for warm drinks became more important, and the protest was short-lived.

There were many amusing episodes relating to our time at Ochilview, but some are beyond reporting here to protect the innocent and no doubt the personalities involved are still in fear of retribution. Robert and Jimmy, as ever, extolled the virtues of a free coffee and pie, but one thing that worried them more than anything else was the loss of a match ball hoofed, for the want of a better term, out of the ground. The Scottish Football League at the time allocated just enough balls for each club at the start of the season, and the loss of a single ball in real terms was around fifty pounds, and whenever the ball went over the stand, a stampede of fans, boardroom staff, security, and even players would ensue to recover the wayward bag of wind. To physically lose a ball was careless; two alerted the chairman; and any more would seriously impact on the club's finances. It seems trivial in a game today awash with sponsorship cash, but such was the state of the game in Scotland, and to this day, there is still a major imbalance in wealth across the various leagues, more so north of the border in Scotland.

I proved to be an entertainment to the crowd one Saturday afternoon. The game against Montrose was by any measure poor in the extreme, with the wind and rain lashing across the Ochilview pitch, and the chance of a goal at either end was less likely than Jimmy paying for a coffee; the Montrose striker decided to shoot from distance, and the ball sailed high over the goal into and on top of the five-aside pens adjacent to the main pitch. The ball had nestled snugly in the centre of the nets covering the enclosure, and as I was engaged in conversation with the safety officer, Danny decided there was nothing to lose watching the game and trotted around the pitch.

There is a method involving a metal pole to tip the ball along the topside of the nets to a convenient hole for it to drop through. I knew all this but had not judged the strength of the wind, and the image of a club board member in suit and tie making a complete arse of things was not lost on the supporters from both teams, who had decided the game was that bad, watching me was a better form of entertainment. The cheer as the ball eventually fell through the hole was louder than any goal celebration, and the episode even made the Sunday sports papers; suffice to say, my ball-retrieving skills were given a poor rating, and for weeks afterwards, I would shy away if the ball left the park.

About balls and football in general at Ochilview, the parent club Stenhousemuir did not always enjoy the warm relations of the homeowners surrounding the compact ground. One house backed onto the main stand, and the owners made no secret of the fact that the club was not wanted and openly despised. The mere fact that the ground had been there long before their modest abode was lost on them, and they took great delight in confiscating any ball which landed in their garden. Repeated requests even from the youth team boys and girls were declined, and 'Bugger off or the dog will nab you' was the order of the day. The vast collection of balls was clearly to be seen through the slats in their fence, as was the exceptionally large mongrel that did not inspire anyone in their right mind to climb over.

I knew my time would come, and one afternoon, giving an unnamed Shire fan a lift home, I noticed that workmen were digging up the road outside the front of the subject house and had taken a large section of the fence out. Fortune favours the brave, and the gamble of a dog being locked up inside due to no fence and no cars in the drive meant only one thing: repatriation, we will call it. Keeping a salient watch as my erstwhile accomplice piled ball after ball into the van, it was like robbing a bank after blowing a hole in the wall. I can only imagine the indignation of the homeowners, but seriously, if you do not like football and sport for all ages, do not buy a bloody house next to a football club in use all week. I have not been back to the ground for a number of years, but I intend to do so if only to see if these people still insist on stealing from the various clubs, because as we stopped later in the layby, there were balls in the van marked with just about every club's name in Scotland. The retrieved balls were duly delivered to the beaming Robert and Jimmy, who must have thought Christmas had come early.

'All players are chancers and disloyal bastards': not my words but ex-Glasgow Rangers player and Manager Ally McCoist. In my wildest dreams and probably those of most loyal Shire fans, could I even begin to think I as the club chairman would be welcoming arguably the UK's most successful football club to play my team, but that's what happened in season 2012–2013. In 2010, Rangers were reported as owing £49 million, including compound interest, to those nice people at HMRC. I had sleepless nights even before diagnosis with Parkinson's over owing the bank £49 let alone millions, but Rangers Chairman Alistair Johnston had to admit that the club was probably likely to go out of business if payment was to be duly made. The club was looking for a new buyer, but with perceived debts, this was never going to be easy. In May 2011, David Murray of Rangers sold his controlling interest to Craig Whyte, who was to pay off the debt owed to Lloyds Banking Group Plc and deliver investment to rebuild the team.

Whyte's involvement became a tale of woe for him personally, with him ultimately being declared 'not a fit and proper person' under Scottish Football Association rules, and the club followed into administration on Valentine's Day 2012. I remember the headline writers having a field day, but without turning this book into a reprise of another club's woes, the Rangers Football Club was rejected by the

Premier clubs and asked for entry to the lowest league in Scotland, the fourth tier Scots Division 3, with mighty teams like East Stirlingshire. I remember the vote vividly, and with Rangers owner, then blunt and straight-taking Charles Green, flanked by manager Ally McCoist, sitting like schoolboys in detention as the other Scottish Football League clubs enjoyed their discomfort.

The meeting was going nowhere fast, even with the expert plate-spinner, SFL Chief Executive David Longmuir, chairing the at-times-open warfare, and in my humble opinion, the tide was turned by Ally, who had asked to address the floor. Standing and trembling openly, Ally extolled his wish to simply play football on a Saturday as a football fan, irrespective of which league, and apologised to the member clubs for the mess Rangers had forced upon the SFL. He openly admitted to being embarrassed for the actions of his club and any part he or his staff had played a part in. The mood in the room was still largely hostile, and I suddenly found myself standing up and face to face with Ally, asking him what he had to be embarrassed about and telling him bluntly that he had given pleasure as a player, and his passion for his team was no different from anyone else's in the room for their respective clubs.

I then cheekily offered him a game any Saturday or for that matter every Saturday against East Stirlingshire, to loud laughter, but the atmosphere in the room had changed dramatically, and I could see nods of acceptance. Charles Green was also very apologetic, more so than had been seen previously, and he reiterated that only one idiot had put his hand in his pocket to buy the club in principle, even if the figure was only a reported £5.5 million. Rangers were duly admitted twenty-nine votes to one nonvote from Dundee, who were to replace the Rangers in the Premier League. To this day, I feel that many Rangers supporters are still unaware of the part played that day by Ally in getting Rangers out of a serious hole, a hole which still beckons today, but at least the club has a future, but only because of his impassioned plea that day at Hampden.

Some chairmen enjoyed the squirming of a fellow club, but there by the grace of God go I, and football needs harmony on and off the pitch for it to survive. It comes as no surprise that one of the clubs who openly wanted to see the demise of Rangers that day is now itself is now fighting for survival, that club being unnamed here matters little openly to a Shire man, and I would never wish to deprive that club's supporters of their game on a Saturday and force them to go shopping instead. Much was said about the actions of SFL Chief David Longmuir, but I have the greatest respect for the man who was never going to please all and sundry but against all the odds kept things moving along and helped people from all aspects of the game to see it at least progress.

Les always spoke highly of him, and often David would single us out to have a chat, not through sympathy but in fairness as genuine football people. His enforced leaving of the SFL when the new structure came into force in 2013 signalled a regression in progress of the Scottish game, in my view; David had been a diligent worker in gathering in sponsorship for the league clubs in troubled times and was never given the rightful credit.

The news that Rangers were to drop into Division 3 was welcomed by many of the clubs, who could see the cash cow of the Rangers tremendous support, but at our first board meeting after the decision, it soon became apparent that many obstacles needed to be overcome, and with a ground like Ochilview with limited access and a capacity of only just under four thousand, demand for tickets would be immense and over-subscribed. I suddenly became befriended by total strangers who just happened to support the Gers, and the media were very keen to talk to the club, sensing a shock result, I could only surmise.

Many believed that we as a small club would be like many and up our admission prices; in hindsight, maybe that should have happened, but my fellow board member Tadek Kopszywa mooted the point that if we up our prices, that was unfair on the ordinary Rangers supporter; keeping prices to the status quo was readily agreed, and the club gained many positive reviews as a result. The capacity crowd on Saturday, 17 November 2012, and a 2–6 loss resulted in a very small profit on the day after policing and stewarding costs, and the ultimate winners were undoubtedly Stenhousemuir Football Club, who must have sold a world record number of pies and laughed all the way to the bank on Monday morning.

Despite the result, the day had passed safely, and my overriding thought as I headed home exhausted was that we had not been disgraced, on or off the park. The Rangers staff from top to bottom had been professional, friendly, and respectful, which was to be expected, but the warmest of handshakes with Ally after the match in the boardroom meant the most to me that day and the realisation that football is a game for ordinary people who just want to watch their team play on a Saturday.

The game in Scotland is far from perfect, and you must wonder, even with the advent of television income, how so many clubs are to survive in the coming years. There are too many clubs chasing not enough resources, and the trickle-down of cash to the smaller feeder clubs simply does not happen. The people with good ideas and the vision to help grassroots football are not listened to and, worse still, ignored when money does become available. The mere fact that players' wages take up the majority of the budget says it all; I remember vividly many occasions when an average player's agent would talk to me, trying to squeeze an extra tenner a week, when it simply didn't add up.

THE HOT SEAT

Being a chairman of any football club is a stressful task and by becoming one, you are immediately a target of those wanting to help but increasingly a target for those who don't appreciate the sacrifices and personal losses you take on. Being the ultimate focal point of the club, people expect you to get everything right, even if you are bereft of resources. Even at a small club, without substantial income, you can still be professional in everything you set out to do, and the importance of cutting your cloth to the available resources is vital if you are to survive in a dog-eat-dog business. Bigger clubs than East Stirlingshire have perished, and many to this day teeter on the brink of joining the long list; without wealthy benefactors, many would not be viable.

As a small club with a modest fan base, there is one thing you need to survive: friends. The Firs Park pitch was a soil based surface and quite simply could not sustain games on a weekend and training twice a week demanded by the coaching staff, and from October onwards, as winter set in, would be sparse with grass and more mud than the Somme barrage. Training facilities locally were difficult to find at a cost affordable to a struggling club, and after using local schools and even public green spaces to save money, the opportunity to use a local private facility was offered by someone who to this day remains my biggest friend in football and everything else good in this world. Stephen Barr was raised in Camelon, a working-class area of Falkirk, and had taken a long lease on the old sports facility British Petroleum operated from the nearby refinery at Grangemouth, the docks area of Falkirk. Little Kerse, as it is known, comprised in those early days purely of expanses of grass and a building in need of investment and repair, but within ten years of operation, Stephen has transformed the facility into a top-class football and sports facility; from an early point, he has supported East Stirlingshire Football Club and many others with facilities and investment, without, it must be said, little return or thanks.

Stephen has worked tirelessly to make all this happen and largely from his own finance initiatives, when others locally were spoon-fed by the local council and grant-giving bodies. Galaxy Sports, as the new brand name, has year on year seen major improvements to facilities for all teams from all backgrounds, a credit to Stephen's vision and desire to succeed. Stephen's support to others has never waned, even after serious setbacks, and today he remains my wingman, and when a joint venture with East Stirlingshire was mooted, the idea was squandered by the club. I knew at that stage my time with that club must end. To this day, I know like most loyal supporters of the Shire that a major opportunity to exist alongside a successful brand like Galaxy Sports was a serious mistake not to take up, and in an era when sustainability in Scottish football just does not exist. It has never ceased to amaze me how any sporting club can alienate the people who feed it, when anyone who invests knows only too well that they will never see a return.

People have asked me many times why I turned my back on the club, and as well as snubbing the opportunity to work with Galaxy Sports, the decision to scrap a youth set-up on the rise was stupid. The direction of any board of directors is to firstly preserve and secondly grow the club, and both decisions smacked of short-term ideals. Having said all that, the club remains firmly in my heart, but the criticism will always be there from many quarters; people forget the investment made personally and the amount of time we put in to keep the wolf from the door. My promise on day one was to not let anyone shut that door for good, and today, that door is still fully open, but not once have I been asked to attend a game (unless I pay, of course, as I have always done).

Maybe I got it totally wrong, but in my defence, I never went against the board, and I remain very grateful for the opportunity to have been the chairman working alongside many football people I respect and call friends, even if we had a difference of opinion on things; that's what football is all about.

Yes, I would do it all again, just differently. Looking back, my time involved with the club was intense, and above all else, I know deep down, my decision making at times went against my family in favour of that club founded in 1880, but I couldn't turn my back on something meaning so much to so many. The club that gave Sir Alex Ferguson his first managerial job is still in being and, I am sure, will still be there long after I have kicked my last ball in life.

Shire till I die.

DUNBLANE

It is amazing how something so simple and insignificant can affect one's life. In my case, it was fitting double glazing to a house purchased in deepest Perthshire in 1999. Living in Faslane at the Clyde Naval Base, with everything on tap, sounds ideal, but in truth, you become a little stir-crazy, and you cannot relax living so close to your work; weekends were becoming so mundane, life was just passing by. By this time, a weekend trip to Stenhousemuir had led to a boy's night out to the big lights of nearby Alloa, a town struggling with unemployment and loss of industry but, according to Ian, 'a stonking night oot.' It has to be said that Alloa proved to be just that, as heading back to Faslane and the base one Sunday morning, huddled in the back of the car, I was acutely aware I had given my mobile number to a local girl dressed in a short skirt, but didn't think anything would come of it; she wouldn't ring, and I was right. She didn't; her mother did.

Having returned to the Clyde Naval Base and finally giving in to sleep after a two-day marathon of being on duty and partying, I was rudely awakened by a loud ringing sound, which falling out of bed I soon realised was the mobile phone perched on the window sill for best reception. Standing naked in the window, I found myself surreally talking to Rose, the sixty-plus-year-old mother of Kathleen, who I had somehow impressed the night before in faraway Alloa. Explaining that Kate, as she was known, was too shy to ring, Rose had been cajoled into ringing me and was very quick to invite me back over to Alloa, saying that I was welcome to stay over if I so wished, on the sofa.

So began my third serious relationship of some nineteen years standing, after having a daughter (Rosie) with first wife, Kerry, and a son (Byron) with Samantha Abbott, who I had met in the early 1990s, three more children were to follow with Kate: Brendan, Fern, and Mia. My record with relationships is very much open to question, I fully know, but for all my failings, I am blessed with five kids who are special to me in differing ways, and as time would tell, their relationships with me as a father would be very different and at times very painful and hurtful, but come what may, I have always been there for each of them and will continue to do so as long as I draw breath, in a rapidly failing body and mind.

In life, specific places are especially important and become turning points, at times totally out of the blue. Highbrook as a small boy growing up will always remain special and forever the ancestral home and a place my body and soul will rest in once my days are done, Surfleet less so, as the Royal Navy lured me away, but Dunblane in leafy Perthshire, Scotland, was the next waypoint in an ever-increasing manic life. By the winter of 1998, having been promoted and commissioned as a naval officer in 1994, I found myself in a job at Faslane I still consider my most influential, being the operations officer for the newly formed Captain Faslane Flotilla or CapFasFlot, as it was more widely known.

I had the honour to work for many legends of UK submarining, including Captain Pat Walker, the grandson of legendary U-Boat killer ace Captain Frederick John Walker, who was known as Johnnie. There is a book titled *Walker RN* I had been given many years previously, depicting the exploits of Captain Walker and his record-breaking number of U-Boat kills credited to him under various commands, but most notably HMS *Staring*. His death in 1944 was deemed to have been caused by battle stress; to be sitting all those years later in front of his grandson and more importantly working for such a great man with such family history was a pinnacle of my time in submarines.

Captain Pat was liked by all and sundry, and although seriously fierce looking and a tall, imposing figure, he was an absolute pleasure as a boss but, more importantly, in quiet moments bloody good company. It is a very annoying habit to many of those around me, but I have always detested being late for anything, preferring to be an hour early rather than a minute late. I am not sure where this habit originated from, but I would find myself most days being the first into the imposing Belmore House within the base, which was the offices and hub of the flotilla, at least an hour before anyone else deemed to turn up.

This golden hour would allow me to catch up on what had happened overnight, and at around 0730, Captain Pat would appear with his coffee cup, knowing full well that I would have a pot ready, and he would sit down and we would put the world to rights, such was the humble man he certainly was. Pat had a great sense of humour and passion for golf, and a case in point was when the Open golf championships was on in 1999. Each day there was a programmed videoconference which involved our input together with Fleet headquarters in Northwood, Middlesex, and our sister flotilla in Devonport. I can remember so well being summoned to Pat's office, where the impressive array of cameras and video equipment was set up. Just before the allotted time for everyone to hook up, I remember entering the imposing office to be confronted by images of the golf from the Open and not the senior operations staff officers from faraway corners. Pat sat back in his chair with feet firmly planted on the desk and with the obligatory mug of coffee was engrossed in watching the golf.

'Tony,' he quipped, 'tell those arseholes in Fleet HQ our equipment is fucked and grab a coffee and pull up a chair; it's starting to get interesting.' A chapter in *Walker RN,* which I still read to this day, is titled 'The Common Touch', and grandson Pat certainly had that, but with great respect from everyone who encountered him. Prior to Christmas each year, the whole of CapFasFlot would have a work's night out, like any other, and in 1998, with Pat leading from the front, everyone with their partners had travelled to the Colymbridge Hilton, near a very snowy Aviemore, and any thought of sleeping was dispelled after a mass snowball fight in the car park and Pat lining them up at the bar. After an all-night drinking bout, everyone in minibuses headed south down an increasing snowy A9 and using expensive champagne in the window washer bottle, finally stopped in an equally snowy city of Dunblane and the Tappit Hen public house for the hair of the dog, before moving on to

Faslane. The pub was warm and welcoming, and noting that the pub had Sussex County ale as a guest beer, I quizzed the landlady about the town of Dunblane which had been touched by tragedy in 1996. She was quick to say that Dunblane was seeing a big increase in new housing, and within half an hour, I found myself at the top of the town in a small wooden shed, paying a deposit of a hundred pounds for a new house yet to even be built, but as they say, the rest is history, and a small patch of mud and Dunblane became a home, at times a place of joy, although lately painfully sad. So Dunblane became home and ideally placed between Faslane in the west and the refit yards of Rosyth in the east, but more importantly a home for the family enlarged by the birth of Fern and Mia, but double glazing was about to mean a change in that bliss.

The new house in Dunblane became a home, and the introduction of stability was suddenly something I realised I had never really had or could remember. I had a base for the first real time that was mine, and friends came easily in a town that had been brutally hurt that March day in 1996 with such loss of life at the school. The only positive after the events of that sad day was that people now seemed to have time for each other. Dunblane was and remains a dormitory town with the railway and A9/M9 link roads leading to Glasgow and Edinburgh as well as Perth to the north, but the shootings had restored the community, albeit for all the wrong reasoning. I was accepted and became a local councillor in 2000, and the community council even thought better of me in making me their leader. It was great to come home and spend time with the family; I also knew that the football club was taking up too much of my time, but I was hooked on it and 'addicted' was not too strong a word. I would get home from Faslane in time to grab a quick meal and would be out again to training, a board meeting, or some other football-related issue. I fully admit I was wrong to spend so much time away from the house, when the kids deserved more of me, especially Brendan, and I look back of course with deep regret. To compound things, Kate's mother Rose was becoming increasing unwell; she was great with the kids and especially to Brendan, who was a firm favourite.

I suddenly realised that we needed to get away on holiday as a family, if only to get a change of scenery, and because of my commitments to both work and the football club, I would need to force myself to go. The answer came from an unsurprising quarter, namely, a local replacement window company, who as an incentive for new windows being fitted to the house offered a sweetener of a short holiday break. The holiday break was duly taken but only down the road a couple of hours in downtown Ayr, but a great weekend with the kids resulted in my decision to take out a full timeshare, which would force me to take regular holidays and hopefully improve things between myself and Kate.

The following year, the excitement was untold as we decided to head to the sun for two weeks in Lanzarote, and a love affair with the island began for myself, which was to flourish and eventually would be my new home. Things came and went at home for the following years, until my diagnosis in 2011; my relationship with Kate crumbled but for a time was hidden from the children, as I spent more and more time sleeping on the sofa as not to trigger confrontation, which was becoming more and more frequent. I found I could not take the situation and in desperation spent more and more evenings and nights in my van, walking aimlessly in the dark with brain racing and unable to sleep. The classic Parkinson's sleeplessness pattern was firmly to the fore and coupled to a fear of being at home and confrontation, something had to give.

I finally moved out of the house; a decision I still cannot believe I had the mental strength to do. I was hurting with my Parkinson's and felt the whole world was against me. Nights sleeping in the trusty van followed; it became extremely cold and in desperation, I even started sleeping in the training pitch changing rooms, which at least had hot water showers, but mice would be regular visitors to my newfound bedside or sleeping bag on the hard floor.

Salvation came in the form of my wingman, Stephen Barr, and wife Angela, who having heard of my plight gave up a room at their house, a kind gesture I will never forget. As mentioned before, nobody can heap blame on another person without first searching their own souls and failings, and yes, I am not perfect in any way, shape, or form, but realising you are mentally unwell is one thing. Dealing with it alone is another. I simply could not continue without harming myself.

> *The fear of death follows from the fear of life.*
> *A man who lives fully is prepared to die at*
> *any time.*
> *—Mark Twain*

THE PENNY DROPS

'You have Parkinson's, Mr Ford.' The big question had been answered. For months, I had struggled with pain in my arms and legs; walking had become a trudge and a feeling like walking through mud. Tiredness coupled with the aforementioned symptoms had led to several visits to the Health Centre in the Clyde Naval Base; the diagnosis had been different from three senior doctors, but the general common trait was I had been working too hard and needed to ease back on my many activities, mainly to the benefit of others. That was just me and something which was instilled within the Ford family. The day had started well, with a decent breakfast, just in case I needed to give up blood for a test. The reasoning was that in the past, I had frightened many a nurse taking blood and flaking out. I have naturally low blood pressure, like a top athlete, but an overzealous nurse taking a whole armful was a great way of getting the alarm bells going at the hospital. I remember waking up once and found myself hanging upside down like a bat, with a pair of female legs either side of my head; a sense of well-being was evident, as I assumed I had died and, surprisingly, gone to heaven and not hell.

The image and feeling were quickly dismissed as a wet

flannel was slapped on the face and a short sharp retort of, 'For Christ's sake, I want to go to shopping; why do you always do this shit?'

The sympathetic bedside manner of my second wife was both entertaining but also unwelcome; having no sense of humour was something which was to have consequences later.

> *God gave me Parkinson's; it is his way of*
> *saying you are not the Greatest, I am.*
> *—Muhammad Ali*

'You have Parkinson's disease, Mr Ford.' Just a few words which were to change my life and those around in a massive way and suddenly, my brash confidence and fearless nature deserted me.

'You can call me Tony,' I remember saying for some surreal moment, but I felt sick to the pit of my stomach and very afraid.

I was worried not about myself but what others would say and do; I worried about having to tell the kids and especially my dad, who had been through so much and now the news his oldest child had an incurable debilitating condition which would eventually lead to a sticky demise.

My wife Kate had physically drained of colour at those words and simply asked, 'How long has he got?'

I suppose it is unfair to criticise such a remark, as Parkinson's is not a death sentence but a life sentence. Parkinson's perception was something akin to the Rotary Club; people knew it existed, but not many knew what it stood for. Suddenly, my mind was racing about all sorts of stupid things, but of higher concern was the future, including work and the effects on my young family, even though I was just fifty. Forth Valley Royal Hospital at Larbert near Falkirk, Scotland, was brand-new and newly open; it had attracted some very talented medical experts, and I am thankful that the person who broke the news on that fateful day is still looking after me. I am indebted to him for the rest of what life I have and others who will be mentioned. Dr Suvanker Pal I describe as the David Beckham of the neurological world, having the knowledge and a passion for his subject which has resulted in better care for all that seek his services.

I will openly admit if it had not been for his positivity that day after delivering the news, I am sure I would not be here today, such was the level of depression. Suvanker is often surrounded by young trainees, and it is clear why others look up to him, as he is approachable and ultimately a friend. It is easy to simply give up on things and wait for the inevitable, but remaining positive at all times is prevalent through most of my friends with Parkinson's. I often tell people that if I had not contracted Parkinson's, I would have fewer interesting friends. Parkies are a rare breed and most I know and call friends take things on the chin and are to the point, fearless, entertaining, carefree, and always bloody good company. I remember vividly sitting next to a lady who will remain nameless at a Parkinson's Christmas dinner and having compared symptoms, as you do; she then decided to enlighten me about the virtues of having a tremor in her upper thighs, which was a real bonus when having sex with her partner. Apart from nearly choking on turkey and stuffing, I realised that she was well into her seventies, so maybe this Parkinson's thing was not so bad after all (I think the term 'unfiltered' is used to describe such behaviour, but the sense of devil may care and coupled with humour will almost always see you through life).

So what's Parkinson's all about? Here is the small print in this book; it may just come up trumps on a quiz night, but if just one person reads this book, my job is done.

Dopamine is a neurotransmitter chemical that aids in passing messages between different sections of the brain. The cells that produce dopamine are damaged in people with Parkinson's disease. Without an adequate supply of dopamine, the brain is unable to properly send and receive messages. This disruption affects the body's ability to coordinate movement. It can cause problems with walking and balance. We have some clues as to why Parkinson's disease develops, but there is still a lot that we do not know. Early detection and treatment are key in minimising symptoms of Parkinson's. The truth is unless you have a family doctor who is streetwise about Parkinson's, it can be months or years before a correct diagnosis is made. My experience is typical, having waited some three years, having seen numerous GPs and health care professionals.

There are treatments that help with Parkinson's symptoms, but currently there is no known cure. More research is needed to identify the exact role that genetics and environment play in causing this disease (or condition, which I and many other sufferers prefer to call it). Since diagnosis in 2011, I have been involved as a volunteer on many drug and delivery trials, and I believe that without research, there is no hope. My closest Parkinson's friend is John Kane, a passionate campaigner for awareness of the condition, and although we respect each other's views, it is the biggest division between the two of us. My last trial completed in 2019 was centred around the delivery of an old drug using a wafer under the tongue and used to counter the effects of an off period, which is explained in due course. Two areas of recent studies have centred on the effects of artificial light and air conditioning systems, so being an ex-submariner of some years, my involvement was assured. Due to the extensive symptoms associated with the condition, most sufferers and experts believe we are still some way off from a tangible cure, but I personally remain positive that somewhere, possibly by accident, we will have a way forward to stop this monster in its tracks.

Parkinson's disease (Parkinsonism) is marked by the presence of certain recognisable symptoms. These include uncontrollable shaking or tremor, lack of coordination and speaking difficulties. However, symptoms vary and may worsen as the disease progresses.

The main symptoms of Parkinson's include

- uncontrollable shaking and tremors, which is the usual public perception of Parkinson's (which, ironically, I rarely suffer from),
- slowed movement, often referred to as bradykinesia, and stiffness in limbs and the lower back, which can be very painful first thing upon waking in the morning,
- balance difficulties and eventual problems standing up, which can also resort in falling, of which I have become an expert at, and
- stiffness in limbs, which is like arthritis in discomfort.

Many doctors who diagnose this brain disorder rely on the Hoehn and Yahr rating scale to classify the severity of symptoms. The scale is broken into five stages, based on disease progression. The five stages help doctors evaluate how far the disease has advanced.

Stage 1 is the mildest form of Parkinson's. At this point, there may be symptoms, but they are simply lost in everyday living; this is why I believe I had developed Parkinson's disease in 2008, but I simply thought I was working too hard. The symptoms are so minor in this first stage, it is often missed. Sometimes, family and friends may notice changes in your gait, walk, or facial expressions, and experienced Parkinson's sufferers talk about a blank expression and seeming unresponsive, but that is not the case, as the person is very much alert.

On occasion, when I have been in an off condition, speech and movement may not have been there, but inside, I totally understand what is happening within my surroundings; I have been seriously annoyed when being assumed as out to lunch when, in fact, I have been totally aware of what's what. The moral of this is not to discuss the individual off, as you will need to justify your comments when fully back on. A distinct symptom of stage 1 Parkinson's is that tremors and other difficulties in movement are generally exclusive to one side of the body. I have always been predominately right handed, so it came as no surprise that my initial developed weakness was down my left side and dragging my left leg slightly, but one year before formal diagnosis, the first indication of something being awry was a major deterioration in my handwriting, which had been of a high standard, especially for a boy. Having been taught well by my grandmother, I was really dismayed when the size of the letters got smaller as I wrote, and the more I tried to correct, the worse it got.

Prescribed medications can work effectively to minimise and reduce symptoms at this stage. My personal experience from diagnosis to date some eight years later is that I am lucky to have outgrown a tremor, probably due to an active busy lifestyle, together being so strong down my right side of the body. And at 59 years of age, I still work mainly in the manual sector, remaining physically fit with exercise, and I still have good upper body strength, although the left side is weakening, especially in the upper thigh area. The only time a tremor is prevalent is when I get annoyed or stressed about anything, and it can be a trivial reason, or I am physically cold. I shake for a short period in the arms and hands especially, but it passes very quickly. I consider myself incredibly lucky not to suffer wholesale with tremors and sudden jerking movements, and if only I would take my prescribed medicines on time, things could be even better. People who do not know me are surprised when I tell them of my plight when fully medicated and active, but my off periods have increased in magnitude, and sadly, a time will come when medication will not keep par with my needs.

The second stage to Parkinson's is considered a moderate form, with the symptoms much more noticeable. Stiffness of limbs, tremors, and trembling in most people may be more noticeable, and changes in facial expressions can occur freely as a fixed stare. When I was at this stage, I would become frustrated with the length of time to complete a normal routine task. What used to take a few minutes would now take an hour or more, and the more you tried to get things done, the bigger the time scale. Self-anger would set in, and without any doubt, this would spill over to the surrounding; you trying to instil calm, but meet the resistance of a stubborn Parkie.

Difficulties walking may develop or increase, and the person's posture may start to change. People at this stage feel symptoms on both sides of the body (though one side may only be minimally affected) and sometimes experience speech difficulties. In 2020 and approaching 60 years of age, I would class myself as being at this stage. I can spend longer periods in an off condition and have difficulty in opening my eyes and drooling from the mouth. Excess saliva can be a real problem to me impinging on swallowing, and after a fitful night's sleep, I will wake up with pillows soaked with the excess saliva (medication is available with varying rates of success for sufferers, but I have found during the day chewing gum can help reduce the amount, but night-time is simply a resignation to sharing a damp pillow with my understanding partner). A long-standing irritant of Parkinson's is that of handwriting, which was an early symptom I really missed and an opportunity to have sought help and medication earlier in my illness.

I fully appreciate that we now live in a social media, keyboard-driven world, but even being able to reproduce by hand two signatures remotely the same is beyond my ability. It makes a mockery of checks made by the banks and other institutions, as never would I pass. The other common problem is that the written text gets smaller. I remember sitting in primary school class all those years ago with a classmate called Mark Billings, who whenever concentrating on a task like writing would invariably stick his tongue out, and it would move side to side. It was a great sense of amusement to those around him, including myself, and the amusement was largely not comprehended by Mark, who continued to dribble and gyrate. It seems my amusement has led to a perverse payback, as I now at times I do the same and will often dribble without warning, which is both embarrassing and no doubt equally amusing to people.

Parkinson's can have a profound effect on speech, especially when tiredness kicks in. The voice can become very soft, and frustration again comes to the fore, as people ask you to repeat your sentence. During my Navy life, communication was key to getting things done; during my time in submarine operations in the Northwood HQ in leafy Middlesex, London, using a telephone to call a fellow NATO HQ was largely the way to progress. I would be comfortable chatting to anyone, including some seriously senior officers, government ministers, and even at one occurrence a member of the Royal family. Now in 2020, I struggle to string words together, even talking to the people I love and hold dear within my family, and many a time, the stress and embarrassment is too much; hanging up is the only answer.

I have received some very good NHS speech therapy, and although it's a great thing, and I fully recommend it to anyone with speech issues of any kind, you deteriorate again over time as the human brain seeks to be lazy, and the circle of despair is complete when funding and a lack of trained staff negate a follow-up appointment. The facial distortion can be controlled for most, but personally, I have found it difficult to sustain opening of my eyes; walking into a lamppost is a distressing experience, but the biggest issue is avoiding fellow pedestrians, who simply think you are drunk as you bump into them.

Most people with stage 2 Parkinson's can still live alone and successfully if you adapt your lifestyle to suit your symptoms, but it is difficult to plan your day with any confidence, as you cannot predict with any accuracy your next off period, when life has to go on hold until you have ridden out that period of turmoil. Menial tasks I have found take a little longer than they once did, but your independence of living is still there; I have learnt to keep one eye on the clock, as the concept of time is often lost. The biggest factor against independence is that of driving. With an unknown time of wobble, you can be safe one minute behind the wheel but totally unable to control a vehicle the next, and honest self-discipline and risk assessment must be to the fore. The progression from stage 1 to stage 2 can take months or even years, and there is no way to predict individual progression. Logical points of progression are not self-evident.

Stage 3 is the hump of Parkinson's progression. Normal issues already mentioned continue, but added at this third stage is the loss of balance and the ability to become a potential Hollywood stunt man, as loss of balance brings on stumbles and falls with increasing occurrence. Movement now becomes much slower and readily apparent to idle people-watchers and can greatly increase anxiety, as nobody likes to be scrutinised. The instances of freezing, becoming unable to walk with no apparent reason, increase. I am often stopped in the street when suddenly unable to walk by some invisible barrier and pull my mobile phone out of my pocket and pretend to take a call whilst trying to convince my brain to tell my legs to haul arse.

Independent living is still possible, and increased medication helps but may bring on underlying side effects like loss of blood pressure, which in turn brings on more imbalance and falls. This is where the skills of your Parkinson's medical support are so important to get a balance, literally. The penultimate stage, stage 4, is simply a stage where healthcare professionals assess you cannot safely live independently, a crushing blow to anyone, let alone someone of my live wire existence. Movement and mobility become harder, and sticks and even a wheelchair become a necessity. The last stage is quite simply a stage I personally do not even dwell on, let alone want to endure, and that is simply housebound and unable to care for oneself.

At these latter stages, many experience confusion, hallucinations, and delusions. Hallucinations occur when you see things that are not there. Delusions happen when you believe things that aren't true, even when you have been presented with evidence that your belief is wrong. Dementia is also commonplace, affecting up to 75 percent of people with latter stage Parkinson's; it frightens the life out of me just thinking of reaching this point in my life.

Another common symptom that's disruptive but also concerning is the inability to empty the bladder. Some people with Parkinson's find it difficult to pass urine if the bladder fails to contract when required, or because the sphincter does not let urine out, or a combination of the two. This is a result of reduced dopamine levels interfering with the efficiency of the bladder muscles and causing a residual amount of urine to be left in the bladder. This reduces the total amount the bladder can hold and creates a feeling of wanting to empty the bladder; often there is an increased risk of urinary infection if the bladder is not emptied completely. I have found it very depressing not being able to basically take a piss, something which occurs routinely for most people. There are several drugs to help with the flow issue, but again, the real problem for myself is the need to get up during the night and the disruption to daily life, needing to go to the bathroom for what is normally a wasted journey.

Having been diagnosed close to ten years, there is one aspect of PD I have not experienced as yet, and that is one of impulsive and compulsive behaviour, which are possible side effects of some Parkinson's medications; recent figures (2020) suggest only a small number of people (17 percent) experience these behaviours, but it can have a significantly serious impact on the person affected and those around them, especially partners.

IMPULSIVE BEHAVIOUR

Impulsive behaviour is when a person cannot resist the temptation to carry out certain activities. These are activities that give an immediate reward or pleasure, such as gambling, eating, shopping, or an increase in sexual thoughts, feelings, and behaviours. Personally, I know many people without Parkinson's who have these failings in abundance, especially previous wives and my present partner, who although only having one pair of feet feels the urge to own numerous pairs of shoes. I am safe from any gambling addiction, as although involved over the years with professional sport, I am simply not aware how the betting odds system works and would struggle to know what to do in a bookmaker's shop (and life itself has always been a gamble, personally).

Returning to the serious side, there are several Parkinson's sufferers I am close to who have experienced more than one behavioural abnormality and with it associated harmful social, financial, or legal consequences. Compulsive behaviour is when a person has an overwhelming drive to act in a certain way, often repetitively, to reduce the worry or tension that they get from their urge. This is all related to dopamine levels in the brain. To reiterate, dopamine is the chemical messenger in the brain that is primarily affected in Parkinson's and helps to control movement, balance, and walking; dopamine also plays a big role in the part of the brain that controls reward.

People affected by impulsive and compulsive behaviour are motivated to do something that gives them an instant reward. Parkinson's medications have been linked to these types of behaviour, with the biggest culprits being dopamine agonists and occasionally Levodopa. It is important to remember that this is a reaction to medication and not a problem with the person or a personality flaw; the vast majority of people who take Parkinson's medication will not experience impulsive or compulsive behaviour problems, but they may develop as the condition progresses through life. I remain watchful and my family warned off.

THE 'F' WORD AND DEPRESSION

By far the biggest single danger associated with Parkinson's is that of depression; with increased frustration, it can lead to suicidal thoughts and is manifested by any number of personal issues:

- worrying about work and finances
- anxious about the future
- difficulty in dressing in the morning
- general insecurities
- mobility problems
- acute pains
- fearful of the future
- personal hygiene
- insomnia
- bladder pain and difficulty in passing urine
- feeling of being a burden on others

The list goes on but, in all honesty, I can say they have all concerned me at varying levels over the years.

The seriousness of this trait was seen in August 2014, when Oscar-winning actor and director Robin Williams took his own life. His note to loved ones stated that he didn't want to be a burden in later life; he thought that his recent diagnosis of early onset Parkinson's would mean he would not be able to entertain and make people laugh again, a tragedy and loss to his family and friends. When people of standing have been diagnosed, it shows that life can go on and actually be enriched, with the right attitude and support.

This aspect hit me hard, and I make no apologies for being blunt, as it needs to be blunt for people to read into the pain I felt at an early point in my condition and the lesson to others to take stock and think things through. The hopelessness of my life hit me hard in 2013, having been out of full-time employment but still wanting to be involved and working, a value instilled by my father and grandfather before. Things started going awry at home, with my family bearing the brunt of my moodiness, and especially in the evenings, when sleep didn't come easy, and I would travel to the forests and hills with my dog Isla, just killing time or picking up some wood for the log burner. I would simply get in the van and take off at ten or eleven at night, just to get away from the sofa, where I now fitfully slept, as Kate and I started to drift apart. I would end up at the all-night McDonalds in Stirling for coffee at 3 a.m., and Isla would tuck into a shared cake or biscuit.

Somehow, I found solace in a small way just getting out in the dark and clearing a mind full of fear and uncertainty, but one dark cold winter's night out with my faithful mutt, it almost killed me. I had stopped the week previous just outside Brig O Turk, a small village deep in the Trossachs Forest, and took to walking up a long access track, as it was gated. The reason for it being gated was soon plainly obvious, as there were several tonnes of top-quality oak wood piled high alongside the track. This following week, I had surprisingly found the track gate open and the wood pile had been cut to ideal lengths for my van, and for three nights, I had liberated the off cuts, but a fourth night was one too far.

It was around 4 a.m., and the ice on the side of the main road really should have made me think differently, but with dog navigating, I decided to explore farther up the long and winding forest track, normally used by the timber lorries hauling out the softer woods. Progress along the track was going well with my old van, taking the ice and potholes well, until turning to avoid a seriously large boulder, the van veered and rolled onto its side. Killing the engine, I realised that the dog was on top of me, and the night was suddenly very dark and noticeably quiet. Clambering out of the van, I realised that there was no way I could physically tip it over back on to four wheels. I worried it was bogged down and sinking a little.

Like any ex forces man, I had to sum up the situation and make some sense of things, and the stark reality was that it was bloody cold, and I was wet, hungry, and up shit creek. Worse was to find that the diesel had leaked from the van, and flipping the ignition, the fuel gauge was not good reading, as my only source of heat was the normally very decent van heater, but without fuel, that's not going to happen. With no reception on my mobile phone, rightly or wrongly, I decided to get back in the crippled van, along with the dog, to try and keep warm and sleep to await first light and the prospect of a long walk out back to the main road some miles away.

The cold became crippling, and I could only think that I needed food and heat, but all I had in the van was dog biscuits and a McDonald's tomato ketchup sachet, which became a gourmet meal for Isla and myself. Trust me, a biscuit is a biscuit in any form, and feast completed, Isla being the only heat source available, we cuddled up to keep as warm as possible. I firmly believe she saved my miserable life that night; someone was watching over me, for certain. The temperature reached minus 6 that night, and the following day as light broke, we emerged from the van to find that we had been sleeping in a bogged-down van only feet away from a very large drop into the nearby loch, which would have swallowed up the van in seconds.

When you are tired and hungry, you think some stupid things, and I wondered if I would be missed, as often, I would be out and about before the kids and Kate got up. The phone battery had died overnight in the extreme cold, and without medication, I had little choice but to wait to see if I was missed or by some strange chance someone found us. Redemption came about midmorning, when two walkers hove into sight and, probably fearing the worst, found one man and his dog. They eventually managed to contact the local police, who repatriated us back home to Dunblane, dinner, and another furious row. The following day, friend John recovered the van, which was in remarkably good shape, but once again, I was starkly aware I had been lucky not to have shaken hands with the devil, but worryingly, I didn't really care.

My breakup with Kate has involved pain for her and the children, and I am sorry that we cannot move on; my wish is simply that one day, we can actually sit down and reflect on better times, and we still have the small matter of three great kids. That you can never take away, but time is short.

I have always been fiercely independent, and the mere thought of asking for help is something most alien, as in the past, it has been me helping others, and now the tables are turned. Some eight years since diagnosis, I still feel the pain of asking for help, but it took an incident and a friend to clear my head, if only a little, as it still rankles, if I am honest. In 2014, as a member of the Royal British Legion Scotland Dunblane Branch, I was involved in hosting a post-Remembrance Sunday service reception in the club adopted by the branch. As was customary, a vote of thanks was given by our chairman and close friend, Ian Balance, the long-standing chairman, and after thanking the masses, I rose to offer the branches' thanks to Ian and, in short, lost it completely. Tears welled as I extolled the help personally I had received from Ian over that past year; he stepped forward to ease my embarrassment and simply said, 'People want to help you; just let them. Let's have a drink. Tony.'

Several drinks later, and the pain was still there, but so were many friends who offered a smile, and that is something not available on the NHS.

Feeling down, suddenly you have issues with working, doing day-to-day things, driving, and getting about, and getting as much help as you can with a condition which is never going to relent and give you a second chance becomes important. I've always been amazed how someone could take their own life, leaving a grieving family behind to pick up the pieces and asking why. I had always seen it as a coward's way out, but all of a sudden, the tables were turned.

The following article was written by Ronnie MacKay,

a good friend but firstly a husband and father who sadly passed away, a life cut far too short. Ronnie was a friend of everyone he met, and when I immersed myself in my passion for football as chairman of East Stirlingshire Football Club, Ronnie asked to interview me, and I readily agreed, as awareness was everything, and although Ronnie was a sports journo, he was also simply a great writer who saw things as they were. I remember him asking if I wanted to see the draft before it was published in the *Scottish Sun*, but I saw no reason, as Ronnie was to the point and never one to sensationalise.

The article is kindly reproduced here; when I saw the full-page spread and read it at least five times, all I could think was, *What the hell is Dad going to say?* I questioned Ronnie several times, asking, "I didn't say that, did I?" His answer was short, and I knew he was right; I did say it, and I knew that life was not so cheap, and the lesson was there and a way to show people what I was made of. Ronnie instilled a sense of education and never being afraid to change people's opinions about anything. A classic example was that most mornings, I could be seen shuffling up to the bank in Falkirk to deposit the previous day's meagre takings, and people seeing me obviously saw in their eyes a drunk when in fact only a coffee and early medication caused the reaction of people to cross the road and avoid me. After Ronnie's article, those same people crossed to my side of the road to say hello; uplifting after being embarrassed, a feeling I still get today when energy is low. It is easy to say, 'Be positive,' but words are cheap, and it is a daily painful reminder that people can be hurtful with just a look and a tut.

3 August 2012
By Ronnie MacKay

TONY FORD had very dark thoughts.

He was in a horrible place and could not see any future in living.

The East Stirling chairman had just been diagnosed as suffering from Parkinson's disease last September.

He felt his whole world had just crashed around him.

Simple things we take for granted like putting on socks and shoes or buttoning up a shirt became a huge chore.

Life became a daily struggle—and that's when thoughts of suicide entered his head.

Ford is not ashamed to admit it, but he received help from local Parkinson's groups, his GP, his family, and his footballing family at the Shire.

The affable Ford wells up as he recalls how he plummeted to the depths of depression in his own personal hell.

Ford said, 'When someone commits suicide you think, *Why did that happen?* and *How could you do that when you have got a family?*

'But suddenly I realised how it could happen.

'Parkinson's is such a frustrating thing. I felt like I was a burden because I did not want my family dressing me every morning.

'I have always been a worker and energetic. Then suddenly, you cannot do up your shoelaces some mornings and you cannot put cufflinks on your shirt.

'There were times when I was going to the toilet and I couldn't hit the target.

'Michael J Fox had the same thing. I was thinking, *I don't want to live like this.*

'All of a sudden, I thought, *What is the point in going on?* and *Why should I even bother?*

'I was getting very depressed about it, and I don't mind being honest about it—I had dark thoughts.

'I used to feel so down about things I wished someone would just hit me over the head with a spade.

'But I have youngsters at home, and that stops you. I did have my marbles left.

'You have to be honest with yourself, and I was sensible enough to tell people about it.'

Ford knew something was wrong while he was working for the navy at Faslane as a submarine navigator.

Exhaustion came upon him in waves, and he moved to another job as a harbour master. Then, a year ago, he was hit by the bombshell news after a visit to his doctor.

Ford said: 'I went to the doctor because at times it felt as though I was walking through mud.

'I felt so lethargic, so the doctor sent me to see the neurologist. He told me straight away before I even sat down. My wife asked him, "How long has he got?" She did not know that you do not die of Parkinson's.

'Looking back, I've probably had the symptoms for two to three years, but the navy never picked up on it.

'I just thought I had been working too hard and was tired because of that.

'It is a progressive illness. Some days it can be bad and other days you think there is nothing wrong with you. You just must get on with it, but it seems to pick its moments when you do not want it to, especially on a match day.

'It is horrible, but I know it could be worse. I've a friend who is dying from cancer.

'One of the first things I noticed was that my handwriting suffered. I struggle to sign a cheque, although maybe that is not such a bad thing!

'But the football family I have here and at other clubs has been fantastic.

'I was well received at other grounds because they all know I have the condition and they have not been condescending.'

Ford feels lucky he has had so much help and, in stark contrast to last year, is now able to deal with the illness.

He added: 'I was clinically depressed, but I got some help from the local Reach team in Forth Valley.

'I also got help from the Stirling branch of Parkinson's UK and Forth Valley Young Parkinson's group.

'They are two terrific groups of people and they have got the same problems having been there and done it.

'You honestly wonder what the point is in going on. I have been so active in the past, but it is like being a top athlete and then losing your leg. It took a lot of people to shove me the right way which says a lot as I am normally a glass half full man.

'It affects your family. One minute I was sparkly and then next I was moody. You would shout at people for the wrong reasons.

'I owe a hell of a lot to two people: my Parkinson's nurse Kay Mair and my GP in Dunblane, Graham Watson.'

Ford wants more awareness of Parkinson's and how it can dramatically alter your life.

He said: 'Parkinson's is something people have heard of, but the biggest problem is simply awareness.

'People know all about Muhammad Ali and Michael J Fox having it, but I think it would take a big-name celebrity here to have it before we understood it.

'Raising awareness is almost as important as trying to find a cure. I think it affects your family. I have three kids, and my fourteen-year-old boy is pretty much a carer.

'I don't want that. When I was my son's age, I was out playing football. I am gradually going to get worse which is one thing I must face up to.

'There will come a time when I am not able to do anything but that is not my style. I want to do everything.

'I get bad days where I just collect my thoughts and take things easy.

'I just want people to appreciate what it is like.

'The one thing that drives me on is for a cure to be found. I would hate one day for one of my kids to have it or anyone else's kids.

'I am here for the long haul. I am not going to let it beat me. That is the attitude you have got to take.' (*The Scottish Sun*, 2012)

I read that article pretty much each and every month, especially when my mood swing was fully wedged in the down position. Ronnie got it spot on, and after all these painful years, my gratitude to him for seeing me as I was and continue to be is immeasurable, but his passing seems so unfair for wife Jane and son Jack; I hope they both take some strength from Ronnie's help to others like myself.

Saying, 'I'm depressed,' is largely misused and too readily describes something we are simply not: merely disappointed. I have been lucky in life, blessed with a loving upbringing (albeit disjointed at times), but always looked after and cared for. Before 2011, I had never felt the need to ask anyone for help for anything remotely linked to my well-being. I cannot even remember being stressed to a point I felt fear or anxiety; in fact, I think my performance during my years in the submarine service under serious pressure was enhanced, and many will agree a little stress is a good thing.

The first thing that depression brings is denial, and I remember late in 2011 seeing my local GP, Graham Watson, only a few weeks after my official diagnosis and being asked if I was okay. As ever, I just laughed it off; my defence mechanism had kicked in, and then I was asked if I needed any help with my mood. As far as I was concerned, my mood had not changed, even after the bombshell at Larbert Hospital, but looking back, Graham obviously knew me well, and I readily ignored his experience at the time.

Within a few weeks, I would wake up fearful with a head full of stupid thoughts and flashbacks to when I was a small child. For the first time in my life, I awoke from sleep to find myself crying over nothing, distressing but coupled with anxiety more than a worry. I just assumed it was the medication talking, and things would settle down. I was wrong; I suddenly cried for no apparent reason and inexplicitly in strange places like a shopping centre or simply in a bar. My reaction to a heart-wrenching news story would equally make me emotional, and again, before, I had been hard-nosed over such things. Anger engulfs me, and again it's directed against myself, largely when things go awry, as normally, I am a little OCD, and if my plan is to change, my brain kicks in, and anger manifests.

I have spoken to others with similar symptoms, for that is what they are, and I have learnt to cope with and overcome many of the dark feelings, feelings that have never led me to actually do something stupid but still thinking of the method of delivery. Having been a clinical drug trialist since 2011, I am very experienced at filling in the suicide and mood gauge questionnaires, and again, a paper exercise, whereas seeing someone who knows you well, such as a GP, is surely a better defence against real depression, which is the potential killer. Far too many people struggle with real depression, but to even try to understand how it feels, you must suffer from it.

Being alone with depression is my biggest fear; with two failed marriages behind me, I am now dependent on somebody who understands the stages or level of mood swing. There is a time when 'Pull yourself together' is appropriate, but there is also a time when the experienced carer knows that the need is greater, and that person should be shielded and protected from themselves. How you protect that person is up for debate, but being able to understand the person and find time to talk and listen is paramount in most people's thinking.

Crying for no apparent reasoning or feeling emotional is doubly a problem when there are outside influences apart from Parkinson's, and the personal day-to-day living aspects for me have been all-consuming. I want to be totally honest with people reading this book but more importantly to myself. Yes, I have wanted to kill myself and end the pain, but I have been lucky being blessed with people who love me through all the pain. I remain wary of my state of mind, and in the autumn of 2016, I found myself on the footbridge crossing the busy A9 trunk road alongside my Dunblane home. I to this day have no idea how I got there, just simply watching the stream of traffic passing beneath me. There were no voices in my head or anger, just a feeling of seeing the pain of my personal life erased by a few tons of a burdened lorry at speed having just navigated the hill and now on the downward speeding-up zone. I could see the faces of the drivers clearly as they passed and surreally wondered what they were thinking, seeing someone just staring into space in the pouring rain. I often considered it totally wrong to inflict trauma on the driver of a vehicle involved in a suicide event, but those thoughts are lost in the reasoning flashing through the brain. You become spellbound and focussed on the road, thinking of the need for timing and ambition to do the job properly. I have again no reasonable explanation why I did not jump but a hand was suddenly firmly on my shoulder, and on turning around, there was nobody there, just a small bird perched on the opposite railing.

I had felt no fear, which I found most worrying, and looking back, I feel now ashamed of just contemplating such an action, an action which would have killed my father.

I have learnt that there is always a door to open to better things, but you must find that door yourself.

Now in 2020, I have been separated from my second wife over three years but still have the worry of personal circumstances surrounding my family that need to be addressed. The hardest thing being separated is not having day-to-day contact with your children and even harder in my case, being in a different country. You automatically worry that every mishap is happening to them, and being so young, they never ring you to tell you anything, which drives me totally insane. Even ringing just to say all is well is better than sitting looking at your mobile, wishing it to ring. It is a constant irritant with my partner, Anita, who is right in saying they only ring me when they want something, but that is like most kids, right? If I get heavy with them, they simply have less reason to call, so again you cannot win, and yes, it depresses me totally to the core.

I know it's stupid thinking on my part, but that's not going to stop the depression setting in, and although I am able to cope, it still hurts, as it potentially means alienating my girls but also my life partner. Something always must give, and it seems it's always me; that's how Parkinson's can get you if you allow it to. Having strength is something I thought I had in abundance, and maybe I have, but it's gone when you need it most, it seems. The feeling of ineptitude in trying to do everyday tasks is overwhelming at times, and selfishness creeps in; you become the victim, and I know it grinds with those you love, but that is the stark reality of Parkinson's and how it attacks your well-being.

My biggest danger is the mere fact that having lived most of my life within such a strict regime like the Royal

Navy, any deviation would cause untold anxiety. I fully appreciate that any plan is a basis for change, but I have always been impatient, and any deviation is too much for me, and my mood will dip. I have always worn my heart on my sleeve, but over the past years since diagnosis, I have suffered more so than ever, especially when faced with other people's tales of heartache. I struggle to watch television documentaries featuring sad outcomes. I know it sounds silly to most people, but that is a symptom of Parkinson's which totally grips me, and I have talking it through, but it still gets me.

Parkinson's has a collective series of symptoms of an embarrassing nature, and I have no shame in sharing here the others in my Top Ten; I constantly suffer with them, have suffered with them on an occasional basis, or have conquered them with self-perseverance or expert help. The number of symptoms suffered by most Parkies is high, and some are quite common across the board, but I could easily name over thirty, which is extreme when gauged against other debilitating conditions. Depression and anxiety are up there for most and followed by insomnia; the lack of sleep and the inability to sleep are commonplace. For my part, my nocturnal issues that have come with Parkinson's disease include difficulty falling and staying asleep, drowsiness late in the day after work, talking or shouting while sleeping, vivid dreams, cramping, restless legs, difficulty turning over, snoring, tremors or rigidity when in bed, and waking to visit the bathroom. Looking back at the stats with my book-writing tool, over 78 percent was written between midnight and 4 a.m.

Some of these problems can be alleviated with changes

in lifestyle, like not drinking for a few hours before bed; avoiding stimulants such as caffeine, alcohol, and nicotine; not eating a heavy meal late at night; and not talking or thinking about stressful things before going to bed. Having never smoked in my life, my biggest vice is coffee, which is a double-edged sword, as my whole feeling of well-being first thing in the morning is improved greatly by the infusion of at least two cups of quality coffee. Not wishing to overly endorse named brands here for my favourite tipple, but unashamedly the biggest advancement in Parkinson's therapy was the introduction of speciality hot drinks served by twenty-four-hour McDonald's. I have been a part of many clinical drug trials but am still awaiting the call for a caffeine study with free toffee lattes. Getting to sleep at night is the hardest thing for me and is very hit-and-miss in the extreme. Clearing my mind of useless clutter has always been a problem long before diagnosis, and the night watchkeeping regime of a life under the waves with the Royal Navy did not make it any easier.

I also believe that my upbringing based on outdoor activities from a young age with my grandparents caused the doctors to miss my screening for hyperactivity. If I were transported back today to age 5, I am sure I would be on medication to slow me down, but in the 1960s, such behaviour was summed up as a child being a little bugger. That said on the positive side, and there are not many pluses, the fact I can still maintain a reasonable level of fitness is down to my abounding energy. Some symptoms of course may be caused by medications, and on many occasions, I have discussed them with my PD nurse and GP, but everyone reacts differently to their meds and trial-and-error (or better described as mixing and matching) becomes the norm, but here's the disclaimer: it's always advisable to discuss any sleeping problems with your doctor so that they can review your treatment plan.

Eating well and getting fresh air and exercise during the day is a big help in getting better sleep; working yourself into total exhaustion does not guarantee sleep, even when Parkinson's is involved. Sleep patterns also go out of the window, and I consider it a real bonus to get two nights back to back with three hours in each. Quality sleep escapes me, but in a typical week, I am lucky to get three hours a night, split up by trips to the bathroom and raiding the refrigerator for a cold drink. With the advent of social media and all-night television, the dedicated Parkinson's insomniac has no chance of continued deep sleep, but ironically, I feel better doing things during the quiet hours without distraction, save for the complaints of a partner trying to sleep. A quick check of the active Facebookers at 4 a.m. will display the usual suspects, mostly close friends with the same issues.

A case in point was how I met my best Parkie pal, John Kane, a dedicated and tireless worker for Parkinson's awareness and training, as well as a successful fundraiser and campaigner. John is a Cambrian legend, and back in 2014, my football club, East Stirlingshire, adopted an away shirt in Parkinson's UK blue to raise funds for the charity and in recognition of my plight. It was an extraordinarily successful venture, netting the charity a large sum of money, but equally more important, it gave a platform to awareness.

John had seen an article I had done for Sky Sports and wanting a shirt had decided to email the club at two in the morning, being a sleepless Parkie, and somewhat surprised to receive an answer from me some minutes later. John wanted the shirt for a fundraiser he was holding the following night and asked if it could be delivered down the M74/M6 the next day. Being the pragmatic sort, John simply invited me down the road to the function the following night, and we have been the best of friends since, a friendship deeper than most, as we share a similar burden and a will to get on with it.

Since that first night in deepest Cumbria, John and I have shared many adventures and ventures, trials and tribulations, depression and elation, and all-consuming laughter, usually aimed at ourselves. John's infectious nature endears him to everyone, and his enthusiasm in promoting PD awareness knows no limits. His presentations to hospitals and care homes in West Cumbria, outlining the issues of being a sufferer, are an integral part of the NHS delivery and training to staff, and he does it day in and day out, without any financial reward. Before diagnosis, John had been a remarkably successful professional darts player, and to have been struck down at his height in the sport must have been galling (a feeling I know so well and share). Being invited to Cumbria resulted in being befriended by John, and everyone I have met has been a positive in my life, and 'friends for life' is a term etched in the stone of Cumbria.

MY PARKIE DAY

I am often asked what a typical day is for someone with Parkinson's; the easy answer is that everyone is different, and often, no two days are the same. Obviously, there are similarities between people's experiences, and even the odd day I simply take my medication and it is an ordinary day like anyone else, but now, that is a rare gift of the gods. I gauge good and bad days with the amount of time in an off condition, the pain and length endured. I have used a random day in the life, in fact, simply the last twenty-four hours. Getting to sleep is a key aspect of any day; hopefully, some time in a deep sleep occurs from around 11 p.m. until the first of at least three trips to the bathroom, starting at 2 a.m.

My inability to empty my bladder prior to going to bed is a real issue and irrespective of the amount of fluids induced during the previous evening, it's a case of rolling out of bed and reaching for the wall, as back pain is crippling. Using the wall to stretch and catch my balance, it's largely a shuffle to the bathroom, and the pain of sitting rather than trying to maintain balance standing is the lesser of two evils. Currently living in Lanzarote, I am thankful that the Spanish way is to have the washing machine in the bathroom and not the kitchen, and ours is handily placed within grasping distance from the utility of sitting down, and with a wince, the Zanussi appliance of science is akin to a lowering Zimmer for me.

Trying to force a bladder to function is something which is a pure pleasure-and-pain moment. Even with the aid of drugs to increase flow, the sensation of bursting subsides so quickly, but after a mere trickle. I have tried all the tricks that I am aware of, taken the differing drinks on offer, and tried abstaining from alcohol and even my beloved coffee, but it is a forlorn gesture. Getting back to bed and even hoping for renewed sleep is always difficult, and with brain racing with troublesome thoughts normally centred on concerns with my kids, I usually end up in the kitchen and front room for at least an hour or two, with rolling Sky News for company and trying to avoid turning on the kettle.

There have been times when I have dozed on the sofa, and fitful sleep has ensued, but often it is a case of watching the sunrise, albeit spectacular, outside of the window. On the odd occasion I have made it back to bed, often chastised by my partner Anita, but rarely to sleep and the surfing of various iPhone apps again with even more news to absorb, which hasn't really changed in the last few hours. I am acutely aware of stimulating the brain more to stop sleep, but it's the proverbial runaway train; nothing is going to stop until the buffers are hit at 0600 and the body clicking firmly from restlessness to totally wide awake.

I am fearful of the night; it is when my mood dips, and naturally, the body wants to slow down, and for a

Parkie, that is slowing down even more. Pain, especially in the legs and lower back, makes finding a comfortable spot on the bed exceedingly difficult, and no number of pillows and cushions seems to help me. Getting dressed first thing is the next challenge, but to really manage, the priority is to take the required medication and wash it down with a coffee. I am lucky in that I can readily take medication without too many side effects; even taking prescribed painkillers is reasonably simple and kick in within thirty minutes.

Balance is the biggest obstacle in getting dressed; a perch is required for the likes of socks and shoes. I do not subscribe to slip-on shoes; I hated them with a passion well before my diagnosis, and normally, with a suitable shoehorn, I can still manage unaided. Within an hour of getting dressed, the most positive part of my day is feeding myself, a task without any issues, and I retain a great appetite. The rest of the morning is by far my best period of most days, with maximum medication and energy, before the 1400 dip in energy levels and tiredness can set in and the dreaded off period is most likely; when it occurs is anyone's guess, but such is the frustration of Parkinson's.

My most likely period for a wobble is from around 1600 until 2000, which can be problematic if anything is arranged in the evening, such as going out to an event or entertaining guests. Most of my close friends have seen me at my best and moreover my worst and accept it, as they have come to see me struggle more and more over the years. Am I still embarrassed being in a mess in public? Yes, I am, and no matter what words of comfort are forthcoming, I still want the ground to open and swallow me. A quiet night in simply watching the TV is the preferred evening activity, but I stress when my partner goes to bed around 2200 and I am invited to do similar. By 2200, I am in full brain rush mode, and I simply know going to bed too early is going to be an epic fail.

Even if I am physically tired, I often find it hard to settle and will on occasion simply enjoy the peace of sitting on the sofa and dozing. During this time, I am at least resting, and I consider this period especially important for winding down. So, is it humanly possible to survive on four to five hours of sleep? It would appear so. It has been well documented that when serving as prime minister, Margaret Thatcher got by on around five hours of sleep a night, when the average for normal people is around eight. I can only imagine what that feels like. I mentioned before that I have always worked in shifts or have been subject to call out, so living a life largely on edge. I have also been blessed with good stamina, but as I get older, I am acutely aware I cannot keep dipping into my energy reserves, as they are diminishing faster than I can recharge.

During the morning, I can manage to do most physical tasks with good muscle definition of someone in their fifties; I even manage to drive. Driving is something I have in honesty pushed the boundaries on, and confidence has dwindled a little in my abilities when out driving over the last three years; to my family and friends who I have frightened behind the wheel, I apologise. The need to constantly risk-assess the safety of driving with progressive Parkinson's is becoming problematic, as the speed of going from on to off without warning has left me stranded and requiring the assistance of Anita to pick me up. Losing the independence of owning a car would be a serious blow to my busy lifestyle, and I hope to continue driving if accepted for deep brain stimulation (DBS) brain surgery. The choice will be decided for me, I feel sure, and honesty must be the real driver of any vehicle.

LIVING IN EXILE: THE END OF THE ROAD? FEBRUARY 2020

The big question remains, will anyone read the book? Baring your soul to the public is never easy and even harder to those friends who have helped you and continue to do so; it's even harder for those who still doubt you. As I prepare for life-changing surgery, I need to make peace with some family members; my fear is that I will simply die before I can make my peace with them. Parkinson's know no boundaries; some take it in their stride, and others simply struggle. Personally, getting older and more dependent on people is hard for me, and all I wish for is a world free of pain. Every day, the physical and mental pain becomes harder to bear, and dark moods resurface, but just for a brief moment in time, I am transported back to that carefree small boy in short trousers with my nan pressing my hand and self-pity removed. I know she would never let me quit but tell me to stand up for the truth, and people will back you.

The simple fact that people do fall out in life is very common and something they may understand one day, when things don't go to plan in their own lives, but personally, though badly hurt by events, I bear no malice to anyone and firmly believe people can learn to accept the past, move on, and even talk without further conflict. My only wish is to see my children make successful lives for themselves, just like anyone else would, and for myself to be a part of that process, but my time is limited. I know that. I am currently living in Lanzarote as a UK resident to help enable the benefits of the warmer climate to quell my Parkinson's; with my condition deteriorating, staying positive is becoming harder, but that is what life is about.

LIVING RATHER THAN EXISTING

In September 2019, I was accepted in principle for deep brain stimulation to help check my rapidly progressing Parkinson's condition; I have a renewed chance, and a chance I am not afraid of taking, but obviously like any surgery, it involves risks. I am hoping it will help my speech, which is becoming harder to understand, with a stammer prominent. To understand the process of DBS, one cannot merely rely on a quick internet search, as some definitions are diverse and ultimately incorrect, thank God.

In short, the head is positioned in a frame to keep it still during the procedure, and a general anaesthetic is given to place thin wire leads with electrodes into the brain. The leads are connected to a pulse generator containing long-life batteries and placed under the skin in the chest. The operation will take place in Glasgow, and the amazing thing is that you are awakened halfway through the procedure to check the positioning. The surgery is expensive and requires a great deal of fine-tuning; I am fully aware of the risks, but it's a chance to weigh up my options, and they are running out, so I pray I get the green light in 2021. I had to appear before an assessment panel for suitability along with three others; waiting for the panel's decision is akin to waiting outside the headmaster's office.

Nervous chats between the four of us and our partners gave way to elation as I was given the good news first, but sadly, the others missed out. My elation walking back to the car was checked by a feeling of sadness for the others, who took disappointment in such a dignified manner, and by the time we hit the motorway heading to Dunblane, I had vowed to try that much harder to help find a cure or at least to progress treatments before my time was done. The relief of getting a positive assessment was probably felt more by Anita, my long-suffering partner and carer, who had started the day apologising to the doctors for my hyperactive state, as I had been given the wrong guidance for the day and had not taken my prescribed medication but instead had opted for a couple of large toffee latte coffees on the way into the city of Glasgow. Bouncing around the waiting room on a caffeine-induced high, things were about to get even worse as I sat in front of the panel, talking nonstop and fidgeting. Anita had been convinced the outcome was going to be a negative one, but I am grateful to the staff at Queen Elizabeth University Hospital Neurological Department for having pity on me (or simply a great sense of humour).

So, the final chapter? I would like to hope not, but whatever the future brings, I have no case for complaint; as I have said before, I have been lucky in life. Good people have loved and guided me. Yes, I have unfinished business and peace to make with many, including family who believe I have failed them, but I remain a father who loves his children and misses them each day and will always be there.

I am stronger today for all that has gone before, although I still know I need to love myself again. My advice to those detractors who doubt me is to get out of my bloody way and take a long hard look in the mirror and face up to their own failings.

**Lieutenant Commander Anthony John Ford (C037629J)
Service Record**

■ **New Entry Training**
HMS *Raleigh*, 2 August 1977–April 1978
Junior Radio Operator (Top Student Award)
Second Class

■ **Communications Training**
HMS *Mercury*, April 1978–October 1978
(Awarded Commander-in-Chief's citation)

■ **Sea Service**
HMS *Sceptre*, October 1978–July 1981
(Awarded Submariners Badge, November 1978)

HMS *Alliance*, July 1981–December 1981
(HMS *Dolphin*) Crew Training Duties

HMS *Splendid*, December 1981–February 1982

HMS *Valiant*, February 1982–October 1985

HMS *Superb*, May 1986–July 1991

HMS *Opossum*, November 1991–September 1993
(Gulf War Deployment)

Selected for Officer Training
Promoted to the Upper Deck, April 1994, Sub
Lieutenant RN
Nuclear General Course, Royal Naval College,
Greenwich, London

HMS *Anglesey* 1994–1995 Fisheries Protection (Navigation and Warfare Training)

HMS *Orkney* Navigator Fisheries Protection

HMS *Guernsey* Navigator Fisheries Protection

■ **Submarine Sea Service**
HMS *Renown* Warfare Officer, 1995–1997 (SSBN Qualified) (National Deterrence Patrols)

National Submarine Force HQ (Northwood), 1997–January 2000

January 2000–July 2000, UN Service, Sierra Leone Military Assistance Team
July 2000–April 2004, Staff Operations Officer

First Submarine Squadron, HM Naval Base Clyde

HMS *Superb*, April 2004–December 2005 Warfare Officer

FOSNNI Operations Officer, January 2005–2008 HM Naval Base Clyde

Appointed as Deputy Queens Harbour Master, HM Naval Base Clyde, May 2008–13 February 2011

Discharged from Her Majesty's Service, 14 February 2011, after thirty-four years total service to the Crown

First day in the Royal Navy, 2nd August 1977
Junior Radio Operator Second Class Anthony John Ford
Official Number D167542S

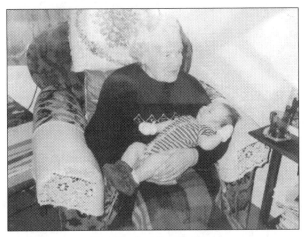

The Pocket Battleship!
My guiding light grandmother, Winniefred 'Winnie ' Ford

Son of an Orchid Grower

Petty Officer Tactical Systems
Submarines - HMS OPOSSUM
Diesel Electric submarine - Punta Arenas Chile 1990

Off to War!
Officer of the Watch —HMS OPOSSUM
Gulf War Deployment 1991

Dartmouth Royal Naval College 1993
with proud father John on Passing Out Day –
My father was the tallest person there!

Newly diagnosed with Parkinson's and
supporting the charity Parkinson's UK 2012

Pedal for Parkinson's 2013 —
Fundraising for Parkinson's UK

Chairman of the Board!
East Stirlingshire Football Club

Parkinson's UK Charity support from East
Stirlingshire Football Club 2012/13

The future? — embracing youth participation
and free entry to matches

Promoting and sharing the vision with
'Wingman' Stephen Barr
Falkirk Shopping Centre 2016

A pair of Fords' — Steve Ford the
Gaffer! from Parkinson's UK

A clear message 2018

L-R Peter Manley, TF, Dave Clark and John Kane
Professional Darts supporting Parkinson's

Royal British Legion Scotland Dunblane –
Supporting from the front

Lanzarote – New life loading…The Sea, a rock, and a cold beer a whole new way of life!